How To Weld
the easy way

Penny Swift   Janek Szymanowski

PJ's
Design Workshop

First published in 2013 by PJ's Design Workshop
PO Box 558
Somerset Mall
Western Cape
South Africa
http://pjdesign.pennyswift.com/

ISBN soft cover edition   978-0-620-55689-7

Design and layout: Janek Szymanowski and Penny Swift
Cover design: Janek Szymanowski
Printing & binding: CreateSpace

CONTENTS

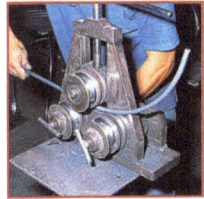

INTRODUCTION

Metal has been used by craftsmen and blacksmiths for hundreds of years to make both practical and decorative items. Over the centuries techniques have been refined, and today it is possible for any competent handyman to work with metal, and achieve rewarding results.

Whichever method is used, there is usually some form of heat involved, to aid bonding of the metals when soldering or brazing, and to melt the metal in fusion welding – traditionally in a blacksmith's forge, but now more usually with electricity or gas. Safety is a priority, and guidelines must be followed.

How To Weld the easy way has been produced primarily as a beginner's guide for those wanting to weld, but it will also give those with basic welding and related skills a host of good ideas that will enable then to develop their craft further.

The section on tools and materials provides a general overview of the subject, in terms of weldable metals, filler materials and tools. Traditional tools are discussed, along with the most common hand tools used today, as well as power tools and the full range of equipment needed to tackle the various welding processes. This will guide you in terms of what you need to buy before you get started with your first welding projects.

The range of metalworking techniques varies considerably, largely according to the metal used and specific welding technique chosen. This relates directly to the tools

you will need; so it is wise to be sure which direction you intend to take before you rush out and spend a lot of money on your new workshop.

The chapter on techniques is substantial, and covers all the related possibilities from basic cutting, gouging, drilling and forming of metal, to the full range of joining techniques, such as riveting, soldering and welding. Those described in some detail are:
• Soft soldering, a process which produces a relatively low strength join.
• Hard soldering, commonly used when working with copper or brass.

• Brazing, which is suitable for joining different types of metals.
• Brazewelding, a popular method of fabrication, which is also used for repair work as it produces a high strength join.
• Gas welding, a versatile, but demanding technique.
• Manual metal arc (MMA) welding, commonly used for joining thick and often different metals, and also the most usual technique employed by weekend metalworkers.
• Metal inert gas (MIG) welding, which requires skill but is versatile and quick.
• Tungsten inert gas (TIG) welding, which also requires skill and training, and is generally considered a specialist technique.

Some of the most common weld defects are also discussed in this chapter.

The most common finishing techniques are covered in a short chapter of their own. These include painting and special effects you can do yourself, as well as specialist coatings and finishes including galvanising and powder or epoxy coating.

More than ten projects, of varying complexity, are illustrated with step-by-step photographs and illustrations. Cutting lists are provided, along with a rundown of the tools (including jigs) you will need to make the items. Very simple starter projects include fire accessories and an ingenious drinks stand. Once you have mastered the art of welding, you can move on to gates and burglar bars and even make your own furniture, fireplace or indoor barbecue.

ABOVE
A cleverly sculptured sun which can be hung on the wall or welded to decorate a gate or balustrade.

LEFT
A simple plant stand made with mild steel bars requires basic welding skills. The idea could easily be adapted to make a table, perhaps with a sheet of glass set over the top of it.

RIGHT
An elegant table and chair made with tubing and flat metal bars have both been powder coated to give a long-lasting finish. Designs such as these require jigs to ensure that the metal is bent correctly, and that the bends are the same when more than one item is made (for a set of dining room chairs, for instance). The use of jigs is discussed on page 10 and several examples are shown in the step-by-step photographs illustrating the various projects.

1
TOOLS & MATERIALS

TOOLS & MATERIALS

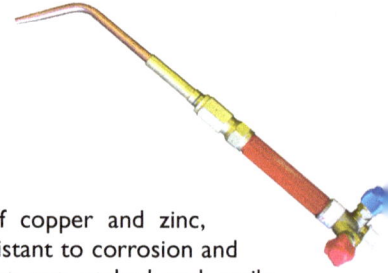

The tools and equipment you will need for metalwork depend on the volume and scope of work you are intending to tackle.

Certain items are essential, while many of the more specialized accessories are optional, particularly for the week-end metalworker.

Apart from various machines, torches, cylinders and manual tools, you will definitely need some protective clothing.

A number of metals and alloys may be used; and you will also need various filler metals and/or solder, flux and brazing alloys, depending on the project.

METALS

In general, metals are either ferrous (in which case they contain iron and are magnetic), or non-ferrous (with no iron content). Both types may be used by the home handyman or DIY enthusiast, depending on the suitability of the metal for each particular project. However, mild steel is the most common type used as it relatively inexpensive and easy to weld (or join) using most methods.

COPPER

Copper is a soft, non-ferrous metal which is easily bent, sawn, shaped and joined. It is often used to make decorative items, and because it is a good conductor of heat and electricity, it is widely used in the electrical industry. Copper pipe is commonly used for plumbing.

Ductile and highly malleable, copper is also used as a major element in hundreds of alloys, including nickel copper, bronze and brass.

Copper and its alloys may be forged, cast, cold worked (see page 18), brazed and gas welded, but pure copper is too ductile (or pliable) to be successfully machined. Many of its alloys can be machined.

PREVIOUS PAGE
A wide range of metal for sale.

ABOVE
An old iron casting, colored green with age.

ABOVE (RIGHT)
A plasma cutter will shear through mild steel with ease.

BELOW
Mild steel is available in numerous configurations such as sheet metal, expanded metal, round bar and tubing, flat bar and angle iron.

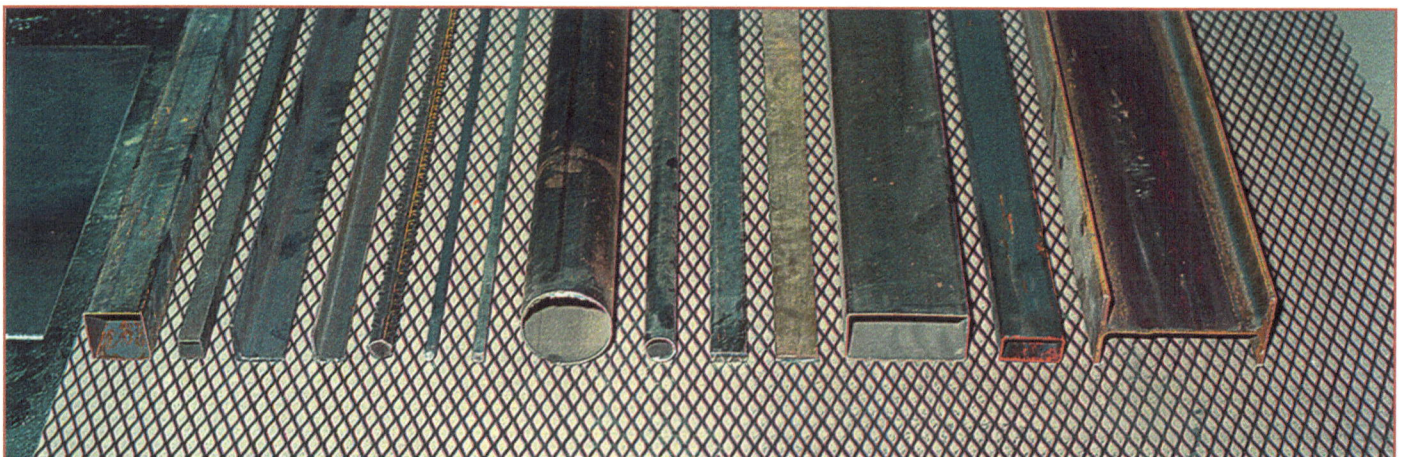

BRASS

An alloy of copper and zinc, brass is resistant to corrosion and can be bent, cut, etched and easily shaped. It has similar uses to copper and is very popular for arts and crafts projects

BRONZE

An alloy of copper and tin, bronze is well suited to casting, where the molten metal is poured into a mould to shape it.

IRON

A strong ferrous metal which has been used for centuries, iron is the traditional material of blacksmiths.

Wrought iron is made from iron ore which is reduced to pig iron in a furnace where most of the carbon and other impurities are removed. This makes it is as close to pure iron as you will get. It was used extensively during the 20th century for railings, gates, garden and household furniture and for decorative items. Wrought iron may be both gas and arc welded, and it is easily formed and machined.

Cast iron is quite different to wrought iron, and is, instead an alloy of iron, carbon and silicon. It is very brittle and cannot be worked cold as it will just break without the application of heat.

Traditionally, molten metal was poured into moulds to form cast iron items. Particularly popular during the 18th and 19th centuries, old cast iron is valued by those restoring homes or wanting to include period finishes in new houses.

Pieces of cast iron may be welded together or joined with other metals to create decorative features. Since it may be brazed or welded using various methods (including brazewelding, and gas and arc welding) and machined, it is reasonably easy to fix damaged cast iron, such as old railings.

CARBON STEEL

This type of steel contains various percentages of carbon and is classified according to its carbon content. Low-carbon steel has a maximum 0,15 percent carbon; mild steel has 0,15–0,35 percent; medium-carbon steel contains 0,35–0,6 percent; and high-carbon steel has 0,6–1,0 percent carbon.

The higher the carbon content, the harder and more brittle the steel will be. Also, weldability of a steel generally decreases with an increase in carbon content.

Mild steel is used extensively in industry and is ideal for general workshop use. It is also the most common metal used for home-related and decorative projects nowadays because it is well-priced and really very easy to work with. It has good weldability and can be bent cold or heated to create quite intricate shapes. Most of the projects featured in this book were executed using mild steel.

STAINLESS STEEL

There are many types of stainless steel, some of which may be welded. By definition, stainless steel contains at least 10 percent chromium; most commonly it contains 18 percent chromium and 8 percent nickel.

Suitable welding techniques are similar to those used for mild steel, but stainless steel is much more difficult to work with and it is a considerably more expensive material to start with.

ALUMINUM

A lightweight, soft, low-strength non-ferrous metal, aluminum (spelt aluminium in some countries) is easily bent, cut, cast, forged, formed, welded and machined. However, unless it is alloyed with specific elements, it is only suitable for relatively low temperature applications.

Commercial aluminum alloys are either cast in a mould (rather like cast iron), or wrought, where the metal is worked mechanically.

As a material, aluminum has many uses, and it is frequently found in and around the home in the form of anything from gutters to kitchen utensils.

FILLER MATERIALS

Apart from the metal you are going to be welding, you will need various other elements including electrodes, solder, flux and various brazing alloys, depending on the technique you choose to use.

ELECTRODES

Various electrodes (or welding rods) are used as the filler material when arc welding. They not only provide a means of joining metal surfaces, but also form a slag cover

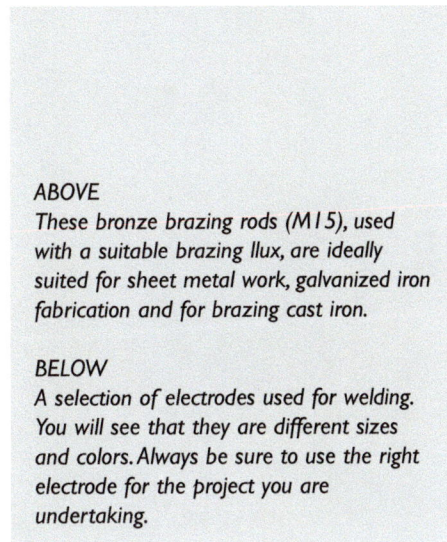

ABOVE
These bronze brazing rods (M15), used with a suitable brazing flux, are ideally suited for sheet metal work, galvanized iron fabrication and for brazing cast iron.

BELOW
A selection of electrodes used for welding. You will see that they are different sizes and colors. Always be sure to use the right electrode for the project you are undertaking.

which protects the hot, molten weld metal from the atmosphere during the process.

The formulation of electrode coatings is based on well-established principles of metallurgy, chemistry and physics, and your supplier will advise which is the correct electrode for the job.

The metal inert gas (MIG) process uses a continuous bare electrode (or wire), together with a shielding gas that protects the hot, molten metal from the atmosphere. It is a fast process that leaves no slag.

Flux-cored wire (a tubular wire filled with flux) can also be used on a MIG welding machine. This is either 'gas-shielded' or, like MMA electrodes, 'self-shielded''. Basically it's an 'inside-out' continuous electrode that *does* produce slag.

SOLDER

Made from various soft metals, often with a high percentage of tin, solder is used for both soft and hard soldering and for brazing. The base (or parent) metal is not melted when it is 'tinned' (or more correctly 'wetted') with the solder, so the solder remains on the surface. So unlike a welded joint where both the parent metal and filler material melt together and fuse, the soldered joint relies for its strength on the penetration of the filler material between the two pieces of metal and into the pores of the parent metal.

The melting point of different types of solder varies. For instance, aluminum solders have a much lower melting temperature than lead-rich solder that becomes 'plastic' at 180–250 degrees C/ 356–482 degrees F. A tin-rich solder will melt at approximately 185 degrees C or 365 degrees F.

BRAZING ALLOYS

Non-ferrous metals, including copper and tin, are used for brazing even when iron and steel is to be brazed. They must be used with flux (see below).

FLUX

Designed as a conductor that promotes the fusion of metals, flux keeps the surface clean by preventing oxides from forming when the metal is heated. Passive fluxes are usually based on resin and sold in a tin. Active (or reactive) fluxes are available in paste and liquid form but tend to be corrosive. Resin-cored solder combines flux and solder and is manufactured in wire form.

All surplus flux must be removed after soldering, brazing or welding, particularly if an active flux has been used.

HAND AND POWER TOOLS

A well equipped workshop will contain a range of tools for setting up, cutting, joining, finishing and for use with welding equipment and other machinery.

The best advice is to start with a few essential items and then add to these as you find necessary.

Unless you are starting a business, it is unlikely you will have the need (or budget) for larger machines including those which bend, cut and roll metal. However, the more serious metalworker, wanting to shape metal, may want to invest in a lathe.

MEASURING TOOLS

It is important to measure and mark out all materials accurately before you cut, drill or shape the metal you are working with.

A steel ruler is often used for measuring metal up to about a metre in length, while a retractable steel tape is indispensable for longer material. An engineer's square (which is smaller than a builder's square, but larger than a carpenter's square), is useful for checking 90 degree joins. A metal scriber with a hardened-steel point is also useful for marking the metal, although an ordinary lead pencil or soapstone chalk may also be used.

It is not necessary to invest in high-precision engineering tools.

CUTTING TOOLS

Various hand and power tools may be used to saw or cut through metal, some of which will already be in your toolkit. These range from pliers and ordinary hacksaws to hand-held angle grinders and large, bench-mounted 'cut-off' machines and bandsaws. Cold chisels may also be used to cut sheet metal and for other cutting jobs.

Pliers and 'snips' of various kinds have a range of uses from cutting wire and solder to cutting sheet metal. Universal tinsnips and other patented tools are used to cut straight and curved lines in sheet metal, while straight snips will cut straight lines and outside curves. Curved snips may be used to cut inside curves.

Hacksaws are ideal for cutting metal for many of the smaller projects you are likely to tackle.

The best all-purpose tool is an adjustable hacksaw. Various blades are available and your choice will depend on the type and thickness of the metal to be cut and by the level of your own experience. For instance, flexible blades with hard teeth are ideal for

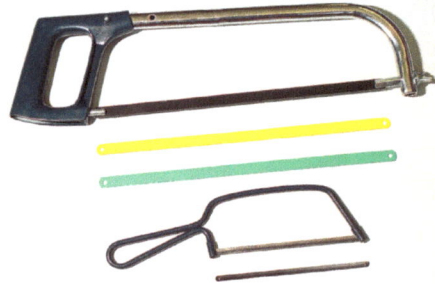

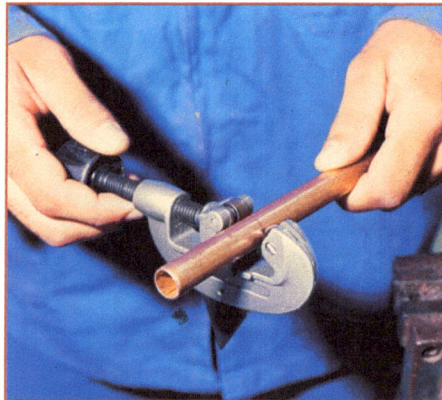

less experienced handymen and a fine-toothed hacksaw may be used for long cuts in sheet metal.

Sheet metal saws, which look similar to panel saws used for cutting wood, are useful for large work. They will, however, only cut in a straight line.

Manual tube cutters are ideal for cutting copper pipe and are generally part of a plumber's toolkit. They are fitted with two rollers and a cutting wheel, and most have an attachment for reaming the inside of the pipe and removing burrs.

Cold chisels, in skilled hands, are regarded as precision tools. For metalwork, they are usually made from tough carbon tool steel which will withstand rough treatment.

Cold chisels (see right) are manufactured with a range of blade sizes and shapes, four of which are most useful for the home workshop — flat, half-round, diamond-shaped, and narrow cross-cut. The flat blade is the most common and may be used for shearing metal held in a vice; for cutting sheet metal on a block; and for dressing metal surfaces. This blade may also be used for cutting off rivet heads, nuts

TOP
A square and a tape for measuring; and a screwdriver may also be used for a scriber., to mark measurements

CENTER
A hacksaw and junior hacksaw.; both are equally useful tools

ABOVE
A hand-held tube cutter is perfect for slicing copper pipe.

RIGHT
A metal mitre saw for cutting precise angles..

and bolts. A half-round chisel blade is used for making grooves and channels, while a diamond-shaped blade will cut sharp corners and is particularly useful whenever you have to make square-shaped holes or cut slots.

Angle grinders fitted with a cutting disc, will cut more quickly and usually more efficiently than a hand saw, when working with thicker, heavier gauge metal. You can also use an angle grinder to grind metal and remove rust.

Various grinder models are available. Make sure the one you choose can cope with metalwork. Perhaps even more importantly, ensure that its motor is sufficiently powerful to deal with the metal you are working with.

Metal-cutting bandsaws and 'cut-off' machines, mounted on the workbench, are another option for those who plan to do metalwork frequently.

Drill attachments include tank cutters which are used on a drill with a low-speed setting, and cone cutters, which are useful for cutting thin metal and making holes.

DRILLS
While engineering workshops often use pillar drilling machine, most two-speed or

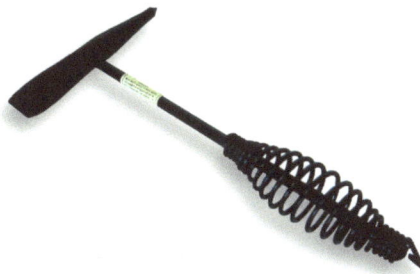

variable-speed electric drills are suitable for drilling metal. Single-speed drills run too fast for most bits and will tend to blunt them, so if you already have a drill, make sure it is suitable for the projects you intend to tackle.

In addition to the drill, you will need a selection of high speed drill bits (2 mm–10 mm/ .078 in–.393 in will cover most requirements).

Various drill attachments and accessories will extend the usefulness of your drill. In addition to those which enable you to cut (see drill attachments, above), metal sanding discs and rigid rubber discs, used with a cover for polishing, are both useful. Grinding wheels and stones may be used to sharpen tools and drill bits and for finishing rough edges.

For the sake of accuracy, you should invest in a drill stand which can be fixed onto your workbench.

HAMMERS
Traditionally, an engineer's ball peen hammer is regarded as one of the metalworkers most versatile tools, and it is

ABOVE
A metal chipping hammer is used to remove slag and spatter after welding.

LEFT
A metal-cutting bandsaw cuts mild steel quickly and efficiently. This, though, is a machine more commonly used in professional workshops where a large volume of metal needs to be cut on a regular basis.

BELOW LEFT
A bench mounted bending machine is used to bend copper pipe. These are quite simple machines, and surprisingly easy to use.

RIGHT
Bending bar with the help of a hammer.

an essential tool if you are forming metal in a forge, or using a blowtorch.

For welders, the chipping hammer (see left) is an indispensable item in all welders' tool boxes. It features a hardened steel head with pointed and chiselled edges for removing the slag. Good quality chipping hammers have spring handles which reduce jarring.

Various mallets and hammers may also be used for bending metal (see below).

BENDING TOOLS AND JIGS
Bending tools and machinery range from hand-held pipe benders to large, expensive machines used for bending sheet metal in engineering workshops.

Bending machines for bending copper pipe are made for hand holding or for bolting onto the work bench. Scissor-action types are generally hand held and used for bending pipe (15 mm–22 mm/ .590 in–.866 in), while heavy duty stand type benders are more suitable for pipe up to about 42 mm/ 1.653 in diameter.

Bending springs may be used to bend pipes and tubing. They are generally available in several sizes according to the diameter of the copper pipe - which is the most common material used with a bending spring.

Bending bars and bending blocks, made from scraps of wood, are often used to cold-bend pipe and metal bars.

Mallets and hammers are traditional bending tools. A wooden tinman's mallet, which has a slightly domed striking surface, will not damage the metal surface, nor will a hide-faced mallet, which is commonly used for shaping soft metals.

Other hammers have specialist uses. For instance, a paning hammer has an angled striking edge that may be used for tucking in the edges of seams; a creasing hammer has a rounded striking edge and is used for forming grooves in metal.

FILES

Where wood is sanded, metal is filed to smooth it off.

There is a wide range of files available; start with a selection of sizes and build up your collection as you need to. Be warned that files are not sold with handles and you will need to buy these separately.

Suitable large flat and hand files include those which are 250 mm/ 9.8 inches and 300 mm/ 11.8 inches long. A tapered flat file (that is double-cut on both faces) is a good general-purpose tool. For filing up to corners, a hand file double-cut on both faces with a single-cut on one edge is ideal and safe. Smaller files should be about 150 mm/ 5.9 inches long and may be pillar, square, round or half-round. Each has its own use. Round, tapered files, for instance, are ideal for enlarging holes and rounding internal edges, while a double-cut square file will enable you to file corners and slots. Smooth and second-grade coarseness are suitable. Flat, rounded and triangular files are also useful.

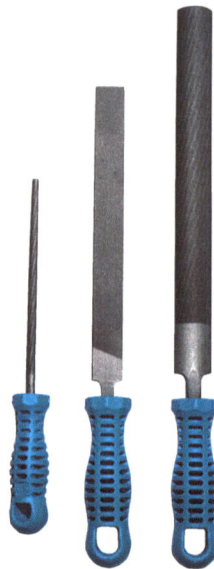

CLAMPS AND VICES

Various metalworking vices and accessories may be used to keep the work in place during the various cutting and joining processes. Most are made from heavy-duty cast iron and have serrated steel jaws that hold the metal tight. Some have a quick-release action.

JIGS

Probably the closest kept secret of any metalworker, the jig is a tool better made than bought. Created from a multitude of items, it is used as a guide for the correct cutting and bending of materials. The problem is that you need to know the shape required before you can create a jig. But, once you have it, you can use it to make identical bends over and over again.

Your ability to make a jig will improve with experience. You will also find that you will look at scrap metal with a new eye as just about anything, even old car parts, may be used as a jig to help you bend metal.

LATHES

Shaping metal is not easily done by hand, so if you plan to do a lot of metalwork, or if you are going to tackle specialized metalwork, a lathe may become an essential tool. However, a lathe is a bulky, expensive power tool which must be housed in a workshop (or converted garage).

Similar to woodworking lathes, those used for metalwork are available in various sizes and configurations. Manufacturers of

these machines generally describe their capabilities by using the term SSSC machines – referring to the various sliding, surfacing and screw-cutting actions.

SOLDERING IRONS

Soldering irons are electric or flame-heated tools that are used to heat a joint which is to be soldered together. Traditionally they were made with a copper bit; nowadays they are made with longer-lasting bits which are often coated with corrosion-resistant metals.

ABOVE
Various files may be used for smoothing and finishing metal after it has been worked and welded.

TOP RIGHT
Soldering irons may be used for a range of DIY projects, including ordinary electric types.

CENTER RIGHT
A variety of metal pipes and rings have been welded onto a metal plate along with offcuts of metal tubing, to form jigs to bend and curve metal to create a number of different configurations. One of these was used to make the curls in the metal bar used in the garden gate project featured on page 50.

RIGHT
A metalworker's lathe is a specialist machine that may be used to form metal.

The size, weight and capacity of the iron you choose will depend on the work you intend to do. Bits vary; for fine electrical work you will need a pencil bit, while a heavy chisel bit will be needed for heavy sheet metal joints.

ELECTRIC SOLDERING IRONS

The most common type used in the home, an electric soldering iron is rated in watts. A small 20-watt iron will be suitable for light work, such as joining electrical connections while a 200-watt tool can be used to join thick sheet metal.

FLAME-HEATED SOLDERING IRONS

The simplest type of flame-heated soldering iron consists of a copper bit fitted to an insulated handle. Used with a gas ring or gas camping stove, it must be continuously reheated during the soldering process.

GAS EQUIPMENT

A variety of gas cylinders and welding torches are available for use in the metal workshop. Although soldering irons, used for minor work, are most commonly electric, a gas blowtorch may also be used for this process.

You will also need various essential supplementary items including gas hoses, regulators, flashback arrestors and various accessories such as goggles and protective clothing.

GAS AND GAS CYLINDERS

Gases are stored in different types of containers, most commonly in portable steel cylinders. Only approved cylinders should be used as these are constructed to rigid specifications and standards, and, for safety reasons, are color coded and marked according to the gas used. Be sure to check the color used in your country.

Throughout this book, acetylene (used together with oxygen for cutting and welding) is shown in maroon cylinders, while oxygen is shown in taller, thinner black cylinders. Liquified petroleum gas (a mixture of propane and butane, but generally referred to as LPgas or LPG - and sometimes Handigas) is seen in dark grey cylinders.

It is essential that the connections and equipment are correct for the type of gas being used and that cylinders contain the type of gas required for the job. To prevent the inadvertent interchange of fittings between cylinders using flammable and non-flammable gases, valve outlets are threaded left-hand and right-hand respectively. Some cylinder valves have threads of a different size as a further precaution. Never attempt to decant gases from one cylinder to another and always treat cylinders with great care. Always turn cylinders off when they are not in use and refill them before they are completely empty.

Oxygen is compressed to a very high pressure of up to 20 000 kPa. Although it is non-flammable, it *does* promote fire — which is precisely why it is used for welding. If an oxygen cylinder leaks, you will not see, smell or taste anything; but it can lead to spontaneous combustion if it comes into contact with highly combustible materials such as oil and grease.

Acetylene is stored in the cylinder in a porous mass, dissolved in acetone. It is a highly flammable and volatile gas.

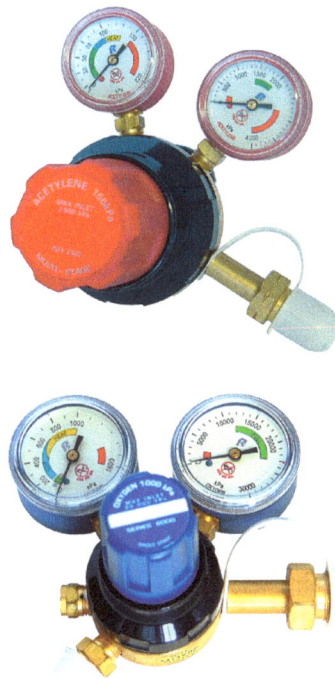

ABOVE
Most modern regulators are of the multi-stage type where cylinder pressure is reduced in two stages.

BELOW
Cylinders are color coded so there is no doubt what they contain. Large oxygen and acetylene cylinders are used for most gas welding and cutting; the oxygen cylinders shown here are tall, thin and black, while the acetylene is stored in the shorter, slightly fatter, maroon cylinders. Make sure you know the correct color-coding for your country. or region.

Safety goggles and gloves should be worn when handling cylinders.

LPG (or any other mixture of propane and butane gas, generally mixed for ease of use in a number of industries, not only welding*) is stored in cylinders in liquid form, at pressures that are substantially lower than those at which oxygen or acetylene is stored. Nevertheless the gas is highly flammable and both skin and eye contact can cause severe burn-like effects. Extra care must be taken when using it.

REGULATORS

Since gas in a fully charged cylinder has a very high pressure, special regulators are necessary to reduce the pressure so that the gas flame can be controlled while welding and brazing. The regulator you use will depend on the gas in the cylinder.

For cutting applications, an oxygen regulator is required to provide a sufficiently high rate of flow at high pressure to meet the needs of the cutting process. Lower outlet pressure oxygen regulators are available for welding.

Regulators are precise instruments which must be treated with care; avoid knocking or bumping them and never open the cylinder valve too quickly as this can cause a sudden build-up of pressure.

* LPG is commonly used in the motor industry and can also provide an alternative to electricity and heating oil (kerosene). It is most commonly used where there is no access to piped natural gas. It can be stored in various ways.

Most good quality regulators today are of the multi-stage type, reducing the cylinder pressure in two stages. The first stage has a stainless steel diaphragm pre-set to reduce high pressure to a more easily controlled intermediate pressure and a second, highly accurate regulator which is adjustable to the correct pressure required. The advantage of these is better control of pressure build-up on shut-off as well as a consistent regulator outlet pressure.

Single stage regulators are more commonly used for pipelines which supply gas to larger workshops.

FLASHBACK ARRESTORS

Gas welding and cutting equipment is safe if it is used according to the manufacturer's instructions. But flashbacks (where a flame travels at high speed within a gas system in the opposite direction to the normal gas flow) can occur if correct procedures are not followed. It is important to realize that they are an ever-present hazard when welding.

To prevent the reverse flow of gas, and avoid accidents, it is advisable to fit all hoses with flashback arrestors. These devices replace normal hose nipples and nuts and effectively arrest flashbacks or back-feeding. The valve within the fitting will also cut off the supply of gas in the event of pressure fluctuations which may occur periodically.

There are various different types of flashback arrestor including fully automatic, resetable designs with a pressure activated cut-off valve and warning device.

GAS HOSES

Designed to provide a flexible means of transferring gases from the cylinder to the welding torch, gas hoses are color coded – red for acetylene and green or blue for oxygen.

The length, thickness and diameter of gas hoses varies; a light hose is suitable for welding and cutting metal up to 20 mm/ .787 inches thick. Quality is important and only hoses that meet national standards specifications should be used*.

Hoses must be checked regularly to ensure that they remain safe. If they crack, wear through to the braiding, or leak, they must be repaired or replaced immediately. or could be hazardous.

BLOWTORCHES

Various hand-held blowtorches are available for soldering, brazing and welding with gas.

A DIY or plumber's blowtorch, which operates off an ordinary gas canister, will heat slowly, but steadily, and is therefore ideal for soft soldering. Some of these

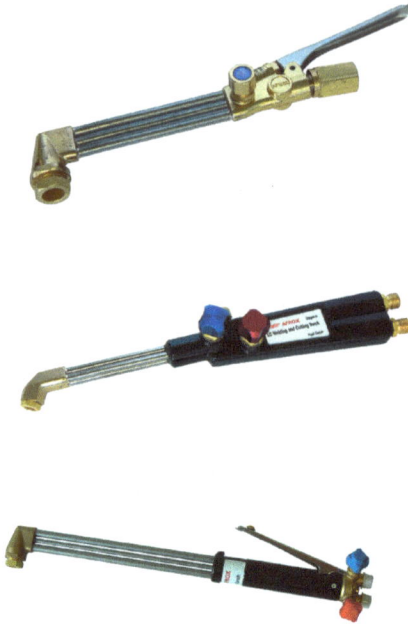

blowtorches have interchangeable nozzles which give a choice of flame.

Oxy-acetylene blowtorches produce a more intense heat and are more commonly used for brazing and welding. Although a smaller blowtorch may also be used for brazing, an oxy-acetylene torch provides more control on smaller jobs and does produce more heat for larger projects. The heat of an oxy-acetylene flame is generally too intense for soft soldering.

Injector-mix torches, where the gas mixes inside the torch, can pose a danger to the operator.

Torches which incorporate a tried and tested nozzle-mix principle are safer, as the fuel gas and oxygen for the pre-heat flames are kept separate as they travel through the torch, mixing inside the nozzle, and keeping the volume of mixed gas to an absolute minimum.

ABOVE
Well manufactured cutting and welding torches are safe, light and robust. A good gas mixing system design will result in balanced pressure rather than a complicated injector system which uses unequal pressures. For this reason it really does pay to invest in good quality equipment.

CUTTING EQUIPMENT

Cutting attachments and specialized cutting nozzles are available for oxy-acetylene blowtorches.

Specially configured nozzles are also manufactured for gas gouging with oxy-acetylene equipment. These have a hard tungsten skid at the tip which allows the nozzle to slide on the hot metal surface and produce smooth U-shaped grooves with widths ranging from 8 mm/ .31 inches to 13 mm/ 511 inches.

ACCESSORIES

Apart from the basic equipment required for gas cutting and welding, there are various other items you will need. Even if you have bench vice, clamps are essential for holding two or more pieces of metal together while cutting, heating and welding with gas. You will also need crocodile or screw-type earth clamps.

A flint lighter is the best choice when it comes to lighting a gas torch. Cigarette lighters and matches should be avoided as they are a potential hazard in the metal workshop.

Nozzle reamers are used to clean cutting and welding nozzles when spatter gets lodged in them. These should be used with care as too much filing will enlarge or change the shape of the hole, which could result in a distorted flame.

Moisture in electrodes gives rise to spatter and eventually porosity and other weld defects. For best performance, all electrodes should be kept clean and dry. Store on wooden pallets (if you've got lots of them) or on shelves, away from the floor.

If you are arc welding with electrodes you will also need electrode holders. There are jaw and twist-lock types to suit the amperage of your machine. The electrical capacity of the electrode holder must always be greater than the amperage in use. Other factors to consider are the diameter of both the electrode itself and the cable used.

Finally, protective clothing, including aprons, gloves, goggles with approved lenses and welding helmets, is essential (see also page 14).

* Note that while the specifications in different countries may differ slightly, there are international standards (developed by the International Organization, for Standardization ISO,) that one should adhere to.

WELDING MACHINES

For the newcomer to metalwork and welding, the range of machines used for arc welding, cutting and gouging is awesome.

There are oil-cooled welders, machines with diesel and petrol engines and high-powered transformers that are manufactured specifically for heavy industry.

For most DIY enthusiasts, a manual metal arc (MMA) welding set is the obvious option for various reasons, including both ease of use and cost. While metal inert gas (MIG) welding machines are often preferable to ordinary arc welding machines (because they really are simple and easy to use), they are relatively expensive and require practise and expertise to operate.

MANUAL METAL ARC POWER SOURCES

MMA machines range from high-quality oil-cooled welding machines recommended for home use, to robust and reliable AC and DC transformers that are suitable for industrial use.

When choosing an MMA welding set for home use, start out with a machine that is sold with all the basic components (leads, electrode holder and so on) as well as a few accessories, if possible.

MMA welding sets are generally described by maximum output of electrical current, in ampères (from 100 amps to 250 amps). This amperage will determine the size of the electrode used, and therefore the rate at which the weld metal can be deposited on the join. Bear in mind that to maximize current output, manufacturers of small welding sets generally keep the voltage low.

Welding transformers convert the electrical supply voltage and amperage to a safer level. They are the least expensive type of welding set available and are well suited to applications where external magnetic fields cause magnetic arc blow.

Welding generators, powered by petrol or diesel, are self-contained units which generate welding current without being connected to the mains. The current output is usually alternating current (AC), although direct current (DC) models are also available.

Welding rectifiers that change AC current into DC, are used as the power source for MIG welding. They are also sometimes part of an MMA welding set, offering a more stable welding output.

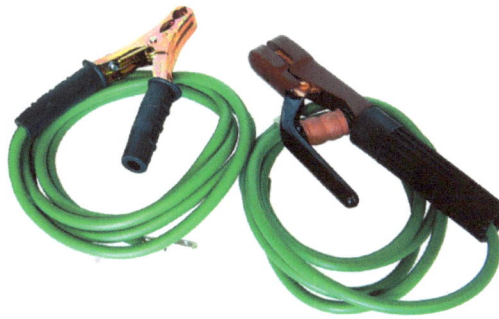

Inverters change AC mains electricity into DC welding current. They have a high current output to weight ratio that generally makes them more portable than other units, enabling the person working with the machine to maintain very close control of the welding current.

Leads carry welding current from the welding set to the electrode which is held in a special holder. Return leads (sometimes incorrectly referred to as the earth) carry the current from the work back to the set.

Electrodes vary in length from 200 mm/ 7.87 inches to 450 mm/ 17.72 inches and range in diameter from 1,5 mm/ .06 inches to 8 mm/ .31 inches. Core wire varies according to the metal to be welded.

TOP
Leads that carry current to and from the arc are attached to an earth clamp (left) and electrode holder (right).

ABOVE
Metal inert gas (MIG) machines are relatively expensive but enable you to work with little mess. Their innovative feature is the roll of wire, housed inside the machine, which does away with the need for electrodes.

Generally the chemical composition of the electrode should match the parent metal as closely as possible, except when welding different types of metal together or when the surface is welded to resist abrasion or corrosion.

Core wire is coated with an extruded layer of flux, and this is generally color coded.

METAL INERT GAS WELDING MACHINES

All MIG machines are welding rectifiers with the electrode being DC positive and the metalwork DC negative. Choice generally relates to the size of current output and duty cycle (the length of time it can be safely used continuously without a cooling period), and accommodates every need from DIY to industrial.

What makes MIG machines different to MMA machines is that instead of welding with electrodes, MIG machines are operated with a roll of wire that is housed inside the machine, and with a shielding gas (see page 29). The welding lead assembly is also different, and more complex. Connected to the machine by a plug and socket, it contains everything to make it work:

- the lead that supplies power to the torch
- a route for the wire to feed to the welding head
- a gas hose that supplies the shielding gas to the welding head
- electrical wiring that is connected to the torch switch and effectively operates it.

The design of the MIG torch is also different and features a 'swan-neck' that enables the operator to control the switch easily.

TUNGSTEN INERT GAS MACHINES

TIG machines are expensive, but highly sophisticated and ideal for industry. They use non-consumable electrodes without filler material, and considerably more skill is needed to manipulate the torch during the welding process.

Most machines also have an amperage control that is foot operated, that takes the skills required to another level.

On the plus side, TIG welding is probably the cleanest welding process there is. On the negative side, the arc produces more ultraviolet rays than other processes. And because you can't see the arc (and there are no fumes or smoke), the potential hazards are greater.

SAFETY PROCEDURES

When working with electric tools and gases, it is essential to take basic precautions against fire, electric shock and explosions.

Above all, stay alert, think about what you are doing, and apply common sense at all times.

THE WORKSHOP
☆ Never work in a building with wooden floors.
☆ Make certain the room is well ventilated. A high concentration of welding fumes can be hazardous to your health.
☆ Remove all flammable materials from the vicinity of hoses and cylinders and from the area of work. Be aware that sparks from cutting and welding can travel up to about 10 m or 32 feet.
☆ Do not leave hot electrode stubs, scraps of metal or tools on the floor around the welding equipment.
☆ Keep a suitable fire extinguisher on site at all times. Make certain it is in good working order. Even though oxygen is not combustible, clothes and other materials that are not normally considered flammable will burn fiercely where there is oxygen – and they can be set alight instantly by a single spark.
☆ Check and clean all equipment regularly. In particular, ensure that hoses are in good condition and that all joints and valves are free from leaks. A major cause of accidents with gas equipment is leaking connections which lead to fires and explosions.
☆ Keep a detailed list of emergency telephone numbers including the fire department, ambulance and doctor where you can see them.

SAFE EQUIPMENT
It is vital to choose the correct equipment for the projects you intend to tackle. It doesn't matter what you are doing, or what method you are using, always follow the manufacturer's instructions.

Never use faulty equipment. If you are in any doubt, replace it.
☆ Select the correct regulator for the gas you are using. It is very dangerous to 'mix and match'.
☆ Never recycle a regulator or hose to use with another gas. If a hose or regulator has been used with oxygen, it should only be used for this purpose. Similarly if it has been used for acetylene it should never be used for any other type of gas.
☆ When cutting metal, it is essential to use an oxygen regulator that allows a sufficiently high rate of flow. Low pressure oxygen regulators available for welding must never be used for cutting.
☆ Flashback arrestors offer total protection. These may be fitted to hoses and to regulators.
☆ Cutting torches with nozzles, where gases are mixed, limit the volume of combustible mixtures.

PERSONAL PROTECTION
Whether you are soldering, brazing or welding, protective clothing and equipment is essential. In particular:
☆ Goggles or a welding helmet should always be worn to protect the eyes from sparks and eye strain. Lenses should be of an officially approved shade and color., and manufactured according to accepted standards.

☆ Gauntlets, spats, aprons and heat resistant chrome leather gloves will protect you against burns.

During all oxy-acetylene welding and cutting processes, safety goggles must be used to protect eyes from the heat, glare and from flying fragments of hot metal.

During all electric welding processes, safety goggles and a hand shield or helmet with filter glass must be worn to protect against the intense ultraviolet and infrared rays which are produced.

The work area should also be screened so that other people cannot see the electric arc or its reflection while welding is in process.

When arc welding, it is advisable to wear gloves, a long-sleeved overall and a leather apron. Never wear loose clothing.

IN THE EVENT OF FIRE
The first aim is to protect people from injury and then to contain any fire and prevent it from spreading and doing any further damage.

If a fire breaks out:
☆ Evacuate anybody who is not part of the fire-fighting operation.
☆ Remove all cylinders from the vicinity of the fire after closing the valves and then detaching hoses or regulators.
☆ If a cylinder is overheated or it cannot be moved, use water to cool it – but keep a safe distance.
☆ Closing the cylinder valve will shut off gas feeding a flame; but if the valve spindle is obstructed by flame, use a multi-purpose dry powder or carbon dioxide fire extinguisher.
☆ If the fire is caused by a gas cylinder and you do not have a fire extinguisher, use a glove, heavy cloth or anything you can find which can be soaked in water and then slapped at the flame.
☆ If the fire is due to a leak from a fusible plug or ruptured disc, the velocity of the escaping gas may project flame some distance from the cylinder and it could explode. Allow the cylinder to empty and leave the gas to burn. Hose the cylinder with water to help contain the fire, and use any other conventional fire fighting methods that may be necessary.

2
TECHNIQUES

TECHNIQUES

Metalwork techniques are as varied as the tools available to work with metal. In general terms, you will need to know how to cut, saw, drill and possibly gouge, as well as bend and join metal in various ways.

CUTTING

The technique used to cut metal will depend on both the type of metal as well as the tool chosen. For instance, copper tubing may be cut with a pipe cutter or a fine-toothed hacksaw. Mild steel bars may also be cut with a hacksaw, or you could use a bolt cutter or bench-mounted bandsaw.

Engineering works often use motorized guillotines to cut sheet metal, but you can also use an angle grinder, plasma cutter or an oxy-acetylene torch with a suitable cutting nozzle.

For some projects you may prefer to outsource cutting. Some engineering and welding works will do this, but shop around for price and service, and make sure that you supply them with the correct measurements and/or templates.

HAND TOOLS
If you choose to use a hand saw or cold chisel for cutting it is advisable to use a lubricant. Most ferrous metals benefit from the use of a proprietary lubricating oil; paraffin may be used for softer metals such as copper and aluminum. You do not need a lubricant when cutting cast iron.

Hacksaw. When starting a cut, work from the edge furthest from you to prevent the saw from jamming. Always cut metal on the forward stroke and if you have to cut it at an angle, turn the metal in the vice so that your cutting action is always vertical. For best results make sure you always have at least three teeth in contact with the metal, but use the full length of the blade or it will wear unevenly and eventually start to jam.

Chisel. When chiselling metal, it is important to get the angle of the chisel correct. Generally it should be held at a 40 degree angle to the metal; when chiselling aluminum, this angle is reduced to about 25 degrees. For maximum control, the depth of each cut should be no more than 2 mm/ or .078 in.

A chisel may also be used to cut strips of metal. Position the material in a vice and hold the chisel at an angle.

PREVIOUS PAGE
Fire bricks make a good surface when welding with any type of equipment, because they can withstand the very high temperatures they are exposed to.

TOP
A flat mild steel bar is held tight in a vice on the workbench while a hacksaw is used to cut through the metal.

ABOVE
A bench-mounted 'cut-off' machine slices through metal quickly and efficiently. Similar to a circular saw used for woodwork, this machine is fitted with a cutting disc, and it cannot be used for grinding. Always wear a full face mask when working with one of these machines.

RIGHT
Universal oxy-fuel torches may be fitted with various tips.

FLAME CUTTING
The cutting of metal with a gas flame has been favoured for decades. It has many advantages over other methods, particularly when you are working with irregular shapes and when access to the cut is difficult with a saw or chisel.

Oxy-fuel torch. Suitable for cutting steel and cast iron, oxy-fuel torches are used with acetylene or, if you are cutting mild steel, sometimes also with Handigas.

Secure the metal you are cutting in a vice or make sure it is well supported on the workbench, and position a steel plate or tray filled with sand under the proposed cut (at least 15 cm away from the metal) to catch the slag and prevent it from damaging the bench top or floor.

For long cuts, it is advisable to position angle iron or a straight metal bar along the required cut, and use this as a guide to ensure you maintain a straight line.

The cutting torch is used with specially designed cutting nozzles which produce a ring of flame surrounding a high velocity stream of oxygen. The flame is used to preheat the metal; at the same time, the oxygen combines with the iron or

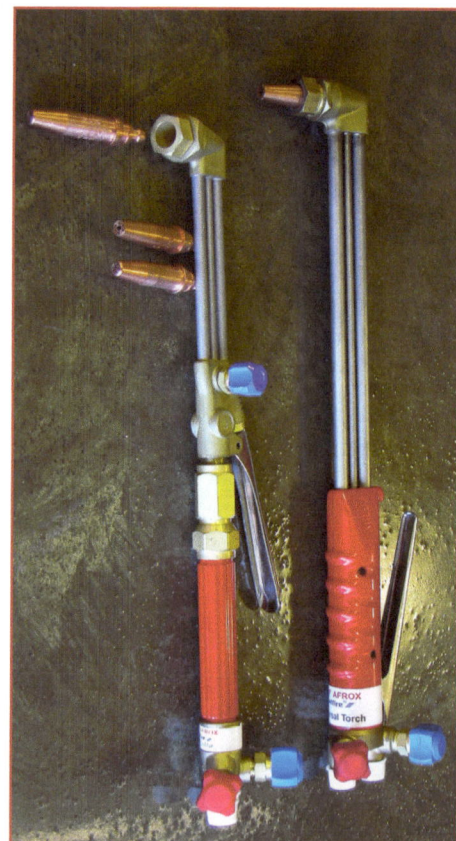

steel to form oxides, which burn away rapidly, thus producing the 'cut'.

Cutting mild steel. The best way to cut mild steel is to start the cut with the nozzle at right angles to the metal and then, using a neutral flame (with equal quantities of oxygen and gas), heat a small area to red heat (see page 18) as quickly as you possibly can.

Move the nozzle to the edge of the metal, and slowly open the valve which releases the oxygen.

As the metal begins to split, move the torch slowly across the surface, maintaining a constant nozzle to metal distance. The required pressure of the oxygen varies according to the thickness of the metal being cut, with a relatively high pressure used for thick material. Also remember that thicker materials will require a much slower cutting speed.

An oxy-fuel torch may also be used to pierce holes through steel plate. Heat the spot to red and gradually open the valve to release oxygen. You will need to move the torch slightly away from the metal so the slag does not blow up into it. Once you have created a hole, you can enlarge it by cutting around it with a circular movement. A circle cutting attachment may be used for cutting large, accurate circles.

Quick ignition methods make it easier to start cuts on curved surfaces and metal bars where the lack of a sharp edge makes it difficult to concentrate heat. Melt the end of a steel rod onto the hot surface just before you turn on the cutting oxygen. Alternatively, raise a 'curl' of metal with a chisel and concentrate the initial heat on this point.

Cutting cast iron. Since cast iron does not oxidize readily, the heating flame has to

be considerably larger than normal. Instead of a neutral flame, you need a carbonising flame, with what would normally be too much acetylene. The excess gas produces a flame with a luminous 'envelope' of unburned carbon around the inner cone; and this is absorbed by the molten metal.

A wide cut is needed to enable the large amount of slag to flow away freely. To allow for this, move the nozzle so that a wider preheat zone is created and wait until the cast iron starts to melt before turning on the cutting oxygen.

Continue working, wiggling the torch slowly, from side to side, just enough to maintain the wider cut.

Be warned that if the metal is any thicker than 50 mm or 1.968 inches you will need a special heavy-duty torch. to be able to cut the metal.

Machine cutting. For fabrication work, where accuracy is vital, high speed machine

ABOVE
A reasonably small length of angle iron is used very effectively as a guide while cutting a thick piece of metal using an oxy-acetylene torch.

LEFT
A professional metalworker makes a wide cut in metal using a heavy duty cutting torch. Sparks will inevitably fly, which is why it is essential for anyone who is cutting or welding metal to be sure to wear protective goggles, and gloves, as well as all the other necessary personal protective clothing (PPC).

cutting is preferable. The actual cutting process is the same; the skill is in the set-up of the machine and use of a consistent flame setting.

GOUGING

The gouging process is commonly used to prepare metal for welding as well as to remove cracks and unwanted metal after welding steel elements together.

There are various methods of gouging that may be used, depending on the metal to be gouged, the machine used and the specific application. The weekend welder may make use of manual metal arc and oxy-acetylene gouging equipment. Air carbon arc cutting and gouging is more typically used in foundries, for ship building and repairs and in the construction industry.

This is what the various gouring processes require.

Manual metal arc gouging makes use of an MMA power source (see page 13) used with a heavily coated electrode designed to cut, gouge and make grooves in cast iron, carbon steel and its alloys (including stainless steel), as well as non-ferrous metals such as brass and bronze.

The special coating on the electrode produces intense heat and energy, facilitating the rapid removal of unwanted material.

Oxy-acetylene gouging is essentially a cutting process which provides a convenient means of producing U-shaped grooves. Ordinary gas cutting equipment is used together with specially configured nozzles which deliver a high volume of low velocity, cutting oxygen.

There are nozzles that have hard tungsten skids at the tip, allowing the nozzle to slide on the hot metal surface without being damaged. Used correctly, they will produce smooth grooves of varying depths with widths ranging from 8 mm to 13 mm/.314 in to .511 in.

Air carbon arc gouging requires an MMA power source, an air carbon arc gouging gun, carbon gouging electrodes and a supply of compressed air.

An electric arc is generated between the carbon electrode and the metal being worked on. A jet of air exits the gouging gun below the electrode and the unwanted molten metal is dynamically blown away.

Metals that can be gouged with this process include steel, high carbon alloys, stainless steel, copper and cast iron.

BENDING AND FORMING

Metal may be bent, shaped or formed while it is hot or cold, by hand (with or without the help of a jig) or in various machines.

FORMING

There are several techniques that can be used to shape and form metal, including well-known traditional methods such as cold forming by sinking or hot forming by forging.

Cold forming refers to the process of drawing down, extruding or otherwise shaping or working metal at or just above room temperature.

While items like copper bowls and tankards may be made using traditional methods like sinking or raising, cold forming is often just one of a series of techniques used to create something. For instance, even if you are using one of the welding techniques for a particular project, for safety and strength, the edges of sheet metal should be formed.

The simplest way of cold forming edges is to bend the metal over a bending bar to create a right-angle and then knock it closed with a wooden hatchet stake to form an acute angle. Finish off by tucking the edge in with a paning hammer or flatten it with a tinman's mallet.

Most reasonably light gauge mild steel sheet and bars can be bent cold and its edges formed, but cold forming an entire object is usually restricted to copper and its alloys.
Furthermore, since the cold forming process hardens the metal, and makes it more brittle, it may be necessary to anneal it before you try to form it.

Annealing should be done after the metal has been cut, and before it has been joined. This time honoured technique softens copper and its alloys (including brass) and makes it more pliable and easier to work.

To anneal copper you will need an ordinary DIY blowtorch (an oxy-acetylene torch is too hot and will melt the metal) and a pickle bath containing water and sulphuric acid mixed 85:15 (which amounts to 15 percent acid). Always add acid to water to avoid a spitting reaction.

Heat the metal until it becomes bright cherry red. Allow to cool slightly until it is black; pick up with tongs and quench in the pickle bath (or in cold water). Let it sit and soak for a while (about five minutes for every 2 mm/ .078 in of thickness); then wash thoroughly in cold water.

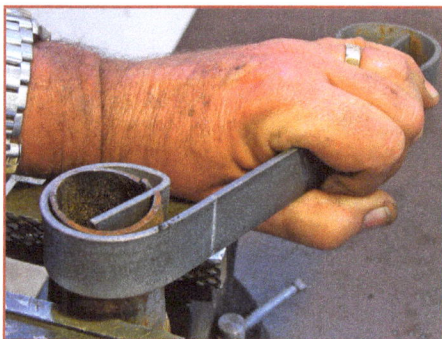

TOP
Flat iron bar is held taut in a vice while it is bent cold by hand. This technique is useful when making burglar bars (see page 54).

CENTER
A stationary metal jig is used to bend 6 mm/ .236 in round bar without heating it. This bending technique can be used for projects which require circular shapes and rings (including curtain rings). Once you have created a spiral around the jig, remove the metal and cut through one side; each of the resultant hoops can then be welded to form a ring. See also pages 40 and 52.

BOTTOM
A pipe is used here with a slot cut in to hold the flat bar so that the decorative bend can be made.

Anneal aluminum by heating in boiling water for about five minutes and then allow the metal to cool in the air.

When working with steel tubing, heat the metal until it becomes bright cherry red and then allow to cool. Do not quench.

Hot forming usually refers to the forging process, which involves heating and working metal in a fiery forge. A technique used extensively by blacksmiths (see below), forging is the traditional method for working ferrous metals.

Blacksmiths use hefty metal anvils to form the metal they are working with. They beat the metal into shape on the upper surface of the anvil, and use the edges and pointed 'beak' to bend and curve it after it has been heated to orange in the forge.

Metal may be formed successfully using modern tools and equipment (including gas torches) and home-made jigs.

HEATING TEMPERATURES
color reference guide

CELSIUS SCALE

Faint red	350 – 405°C
Dark red	460 – 520°C
Dark cherry	475 – 530°C
Cherry red	545 – 600°C
Bright cherry	640 – 695°C
Dark orange	740 – 795°C
Orange	795 – 850°C
Yellow	820 – 880°C
Yellow/white	over 930°C

FAHRENHEIT SCALE

Faint red	662 – 761°F
Dark red	860 – 968°F
Dark cherry	882 – 986°F
Cherry red	1013 – 1112°F
Bright cherry	1184 – 1283°F
Dark orange	1364 – 1463°F
Orange	1463 – 1562°F
Yellow	1508 – 1616°F
Yellow/white	over 1706°F

BENDING

Light gauge metal, including sheet metal, pipes and both flat and round bars, can be bent cold with relative ease. However, bending is often easier if the metal is annealed beforehand.

Pipes and tubing. Some light gauge pipe and small bore tubing can be bent by hand without the help of a machine or former. You can even use your knee instead of a former if the bend radius is not critical. However, you will achieve a more accurate bend if you use some sort of pipe bending machine. When bending heavier gauge and bigger tubing you will find that a machine or bending tool is indispensable.

If you know the radius and angle of the bend required, it is easy to work out approximately how much tubing is needed for the bend. Multiply the bend radius by the bend angle and divide by 60. Before you start working, mark the bend allowance on the pipe – but only cut the straight end to length after you have bent the pipe, just in case the bend is not totally accurate.

Since bending pipes and tubing stretches the metal unevenly, filler material is sometimes used to support a bend internally. For instance, lighter gauge pipes may be packed with dry silver sand or resin and the ends plugged to prevent it from spilling during bending. If the tube is supported with filler, the minimum bend radius should be at least one and half times the diameter of the tubing; if it is not supported, the minimum radius should be at least four times the diameter otherwise wrinkling may occur.

Sheet metal. Small work using sheet metal can usually be formed and bent with

TOP
A drill press will enable you to drill accurately into metal.

ABOVE
A pipe is used to keep the metal bar straight whilst it is being bent.

BELOW
A large machine is used to bend sheet metal in a college workshop.

a mallet. To bend curved shapes, you can make a former from a block of hardwood and bend it over this; alternatively, make a customized jig from scrap metal.

The bending line should be marked out before you try to bend the metal. Use a pencil or soapstone chalk, not a scriber, as this could cause the metal to split or crack along the mark when you start to bend it.

When bending sheet metal by hand it is vital to support the metal close to the bend on both sides. Use bending bars, or improvise with hardwood battens held in place by G-clamps. You will need to use a mallet when bending heavier metal; for lighter metal you can simply bend gradually along the line using your hands.

For projects that use sheet metal that must be bent accurately along the edges before it is welded (including the fireplace and barbecue unit featured on pages 55–57 and 58–61) you are advised to use a motorized bending press. This will usually mean outsourcing to an engineering works or welding shop. Some technical colleges will also do the job for you at a reasonable price.

DRILLING

Successful drilling of metal depends primarily on two factors: the correct tool combined with the right technique.

While various bits may be used to drill into metal, including countersink bits (which accommodate countersunk screws and rivets), twist bits are the most usual option.

To drill a hole, first mark its position and then use a center punch with an 80 degree angle to create a starting point for the drill bit. If the hole is relatively large, use dividers to scribe the required diameter, and then use a dot punch with a 60 degree point to mark the circle.

Before you start drilling, clamp the metal down. Preferably use the drill on a stand rather than trying to hand-hold it. While you will be limited to the variations of speed on the drill, a good rule of thumb to remember is that the bigger the bit, the slower the speed.

When a hole is required in sheet metal, it is usually preferable to punch it (rather than drill); and when cutting into thin metal containers, a tank cutter attachment used on the drill is more efficient. A hole saw attachment may be used to cut large holes in thin metal, but should only be used at a slow speed.

Before drilling into metal, the material should be lubricated as for sawing.

JOINING

Metal of different types can be joined in various ways, most commonly using rivets or with some type of technique that relies on heat (including welding).

Nuts, bolts and screws may also be used, although these are generally considered to be temporary methods of joining.

RIVETING

Rivets, usually made from the same metal type that you are joining, come with several definable head shapes suitable for different uses. For instance, a rivet with a round head is used for general plate work, while a countersunk rivet is used when a flush finish is required. Flat rivets are used for thin plate work – for light metal boxes or repairing items like wheelbarrows. 'Pop' rivets, which can be installed from one side only, are often used for DIY projects.

Inserted with a rivet gun (or pliers) they all have the same head shape and are not generally suitable for decorative use.

Unlike welded joints which are subjected to tensile (or pulling) loads, rivet joints are subjected to shearing loads. For this reason, the more strain the joint has to take, the more rivets will be required to ensure that the joint stays intact.

Single lap joints are the simplest type of joint that may be made with rivets; for instance where one sheet of metal is laid over another and the two are riveted together. Where a smooth surface is required, it will be necessary to join the metal with a butt joint with a single lap – preferably fastened with countersunk rivets. However, a butt joint with a double lap will produce a much stronger joint.

When designing rivet joints, make sure that the diameter of the rivet is not less than the thickness of one piece of metal and no more than three times its thickness.

A recommended rule of thumb is to measure the thinnest piece of metal you are joining and to double this measurement to determine what diameter the rivets should be.

When working with rivets, the most common errors are caused by using incorrect techniques. For instance, holes drilled for rivets must match their size; if they do not, the rivet may bend. The rivet may also bend if it is too long for the hole you have drilled. Another danger is that if you do not hammer the rivet right in the center, it could split.

Special tools are required for blind riveting.

HEAT METHODS

There are two main methods of joining metals together that use heat: non-fusion joining, which includes soft and hard soldering, as well as brazing and brazewelding, and more powerful fusion welding, that results in very strong high tensile joints.

When using the simpler non-fusion jointing methods, pieces of metal are bonded with quite light filler wire (or solder). This is heated to a liquid state on the metal to be joined and is then used to literally 'stick' pieces of parent metal together. A relatively common alternative that is suitable in some applications, is to fill the joints with epoxy resin. This also fuses the two pieces of metal and keeps them together. But it isn't nearly as strong as fusion welding.

With fusion welding, both the filler wire and parent (or base) metal are heated to melting point so that they flow together and then solidify as a much stronger, homogeneous joint. There are several basic,

but similar heat-related processes, ranging from simple soldering and brazing to arc welding, all of which are discussed further on in this chapter.

Typical joints include butt and fillet welds, the latter named after their cross-sectional, roughly triangular, shape.

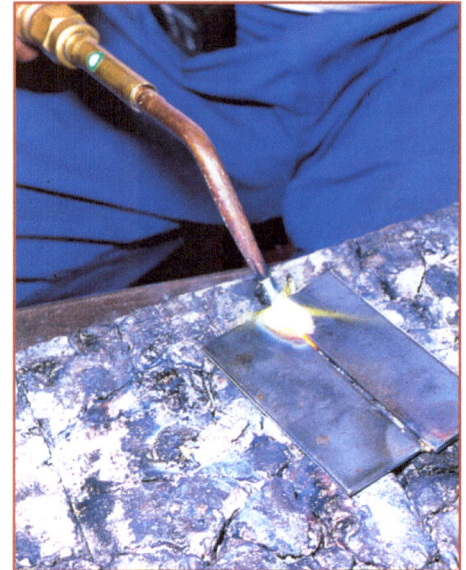

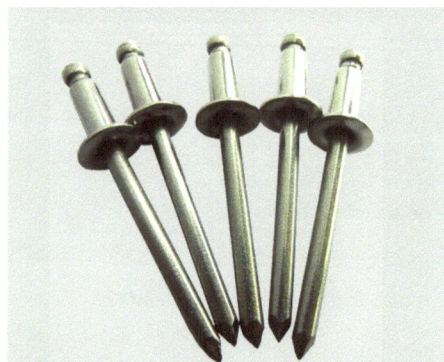

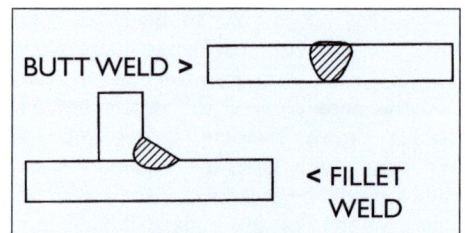

TOP RIGHT
It is essential to choose the right tool for the "joining" job you are going to be tackling. An oxy-acetylene torch is the correct tool to use to braze two pieces of metal together. You must also be sure to use the right consumables with the torch.

CENTER RIGHT
These drawings show how a butt weld and a fillet weld have been used to form a butt joint and a corner joint respectively. The photographs below this drawing show realistically how the welds look once they have been executed.

BELOW CENTER RIGHT
A butt weld executed by a professional welder.

BOTTOM
A fillet weld executed by a professional welder.

SOLDERING

Two of the earliest metals used by man were tin and lead, so it is not surprising that lead soldering was one of the first methods used to join these metals hundreds of years ago. Today various modern alloys are used to solder metal together, but the basic soldering technique has remained the same.

Hard and soft soldering techniques are similar, although different alloys are used for each. The filler metal is heated to a much higher temperature when hard soldering, and hard soldering will also produce a much stronger joint.

SOFT SOLDERING

Also referred to as lead soldering, this simple and relatively inexpensive technique is often used around the home to repair light metal items, such as ornaments. It is not difficult to execute and is also used for some electrical connections and to join copper pipe for plumbing.

Both soldering irons and blowtorches may be used for soft soldering, depending on the job. Most smaller domestic projects can be tackled with a small, basic 20 watt electric soldering iron; the kind you will find on the shelves at any home improvement or hardware-type store.

A fairly wide selection of solder material is available to suit a wide range of applications. In addition, a passive flux is generally used for soft soldering, usually in the form of a paste. The alternative is a flux-cored solder that will give you a self-

SUITABLE METALS
– soft soldering –

brass
copper
steel
aluminum
zinc

---

contained supply of passive flux as you work. As heat is applied, the flux melts and spreads over the surface preventing oxidisation

Before you start soldering, the metal to be joined must be clean. Rubbing it down with steel wool is usually quite adequate, but if it is very dirty, you may need to dip it into a weak acid solution to clean it. Flush

ABOVE LEFT
Before copper pipe can be soldered it must be thoroughly cleaned. A thin coating of flux paste should then be applied to the ends of the pipe to prevent oxides from forming on the surface when it is heated.

ABOVE RIGHT
Working with the pipe secured in a vice on the work bench, bend the end of the wire across the diameter of the pipe. This will give you a reasonably accurate estimate of how much solder is required for the join. before you actually start the soldering process.

BELOW LEFT
Slot the tee-piece (or other metal to be joined) over the top of the pipe. Switch on and ignite the gas and position the flame against the copper pipe to heat it. Be sure to regulate the temperature of the torch. If it is not hot enough the solder might melt, but it will tend to be rough and lumpy, and it won't flow around the joint. If it is too hot, the soldered joint will have a gritty, pitted appearance to it.

BELOW RIGHT
Switch on and light the gas and heat up the copper. Regulate the temperature. When the copper is hot enough, the solder will melt against it and fill the join. Do not allow it to melt in the flame itself. Keep the tip of the solder wire on the join, moving it around the pipe to get an even spread.

---

all the acid off with fresh water and allow it to dry thoroughly.

The ends of the clean metal should be coated with flux and then heated before the solder is applied. Temperature is all important; if the parent metal is too hot, the solder will tend to have a gritty, pitted appearance; if it is too cold, the solder may melt on it, but it will be rough and lumpy and will not flow over or around the joint properly.

Lead solder is weak in tension, which means joints must be overlapped and not butted together. It is important to realize that its function is to hold the metal together, not to carry any load.

When soldering pipe, lengths may be slotted over one another once the flux has been applied, otherwise both sides of the metal to be joined are 'wetted' (some people say 'tinned') with solder. If the surface does not 'wet' successfully, it may be because the surface is not sufficiently clean or it could be because you have not used enough flux.

If the metal is not hot enough you will generally find that solder droplets run off the surface rather like balls of mercury. If the metal is too hot the flux will burn off and the surface will oxidize. The only other probable reasons for it failing to 'wet' are because too little solder has been applied to the soldering iron, or because the iron has overheated and will not take the solder. Since the transfer of heat from the iron to the metal is mostly via the solder, it is vital to keep it loaded at all times.

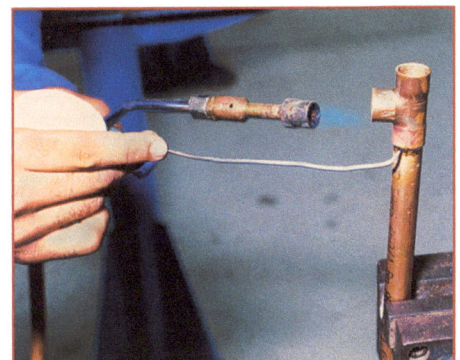

Once the metal has been joined, you will need to fill gaps with additional solder. Hold the soldering iron at one edge of the joint until the heat conducts through the joint and the solder melts. Then, using more flux and solder, move the iron slowly and firmly along the joint where it needs to be filled. While flame heating can speed up this process, if you try to work too quickly, the solder on the upper surface will oxidize before the solder on the lower surface has melted.

Generally, when soldering, the greater the area of metal in and around the joint, the greater the heat required.

Some experts suggest soldering on a wooden workbench, securing the metal to be soldered between pieces of timber inside the vice. The reason for this is that a lot of heat will be lost down the sides of a metal vice or clamp if these are used to hold the metal on their own.

HARD SOLDERING

Hard soldering (also known as silver soldering and silver brazing) is especially suitable for joining and repairing smaller items which would be damaged by the higher heat required for brazing.

Although the hard and soft soldering techniques are essentially the same in principle, the flux for hard soldering must be designed for use up to about 650 degrees C or 1202 degrees F, depending on the silver brazing alloy used. General purpose alloy rods are available and these provide excellent ductility. Flux is available as a paste and powder; this prevents oxidation of the base and filler materials.

SUITABLE METALS
– hard soldering –

brass
copper
steel
stainless steel

When it comes to the filler wire, the silver content can vary from 2 to 85 percent, although it is commonly between 30 and 50 percent. A silver solder containing about 60 percent silver will have a melting range of anything between 690 degrees C (1274 F) and 735 degrees C (1355 F).

When using this technique, joint design is an important factor as silver brazing alloys rely on capillary flow to fill the space between the pieces of metal being joined. The joints are not meant for bridging wide gaps and they do not produce large fillets. Silver brazed joints have maximum strength in the 'shear' direction and joints should therefore be designed to take advantage of this feature (see illustrations below left).

Even though the filler metal used for silver brazing is relatively costly, the expense is offset by exceptional capillary flow and fluidity. Since the joints need to be close fitting (with a clearance of about 0,01–0,2 mm or .0003–.078 in), very little silver alloy is actually used.

Many silver brazing alloys (fillers) contain cadmium, which has toxic qualities, so should never be used to repair equipment or appliances which will be used for preparing food or for cooking. These alloys also give off toxic fumes when heated, so it is essential that there is adequate ventilation when you are working.

Hard soldering is a relatively simple technique to master, but the correct procedure must be followed.

The parts to be joined must be spotlessly clean since the slightest trace of any foreign material will prevent the free flow of the silver brazing alloy. Flux must be painted over the surfaces to be soldered to ensure that the joint remains clean while it is heated.

Use a neutral flame (with equal quantities of oxygen and gas) to heat the joint and keep the nozzle at least 40–45 mm or 1.574–1.771 in from the metal to avoid overheating.

When the metal you are joining reaches a dull red heat, touch the joint with the silver brazing rod. It should melt quickly and flow into the joint without you having to heat the rod directly. Continue to heat the metal and add rod until the joint is filled. Do not overfill.

When the joint cools, remove flux residue with warm water, scrubbing and brushing where necessary.

ABOVE
General purpose silver brazing rods for low temperature joining of most metals in common use.

LEFT
Typical joint designs used when silver brazing

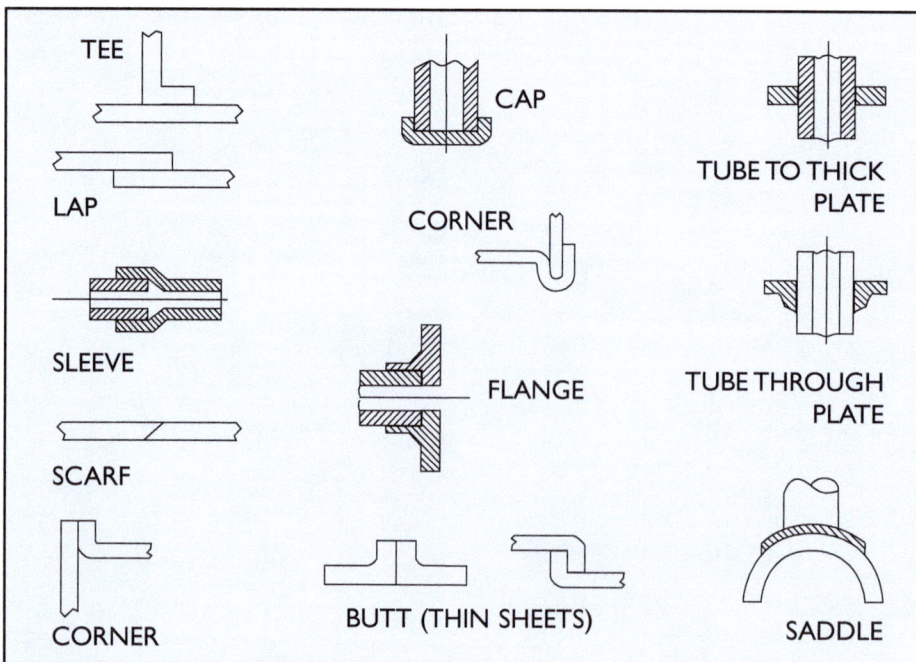

TEE

LAP

SLEEVE

SCARF

CORNER

CAP

CORNER

FLANGE

BUTT (THIN SHEETS)

TUBE TO THICK PLATE

TUBE THROUGH PLATE

SADDLE

BRAZING

Similar to silver brazing, but executed at a much higher temperature, brazing is in fact a soldering technique. However, it uses the same filler wire as brazewelding (see reference on page 24).

The technique requires joints with a very close fit and overlapping surfaces; this takes advantage of the capillary effect which draws the brazing metal (filler) between the two pieces of metal being joined. The parts must be joined without melting the base metals, and the filler material must have a melting temperature above 450 degrees C or 842 degrees F.

One of the advantages of brazing is that it is suitable for joining different types of metals with different melting temperatures as well as metals of different thicknesses. It is used extensively in plumbing work.

Your choice of filler wire (or brazing rod) will depend on the metal you are working with. These filler materials are all primarily brass (a copper/zinc alloy) to which further alloys such as silicon and manganese are added to aid capillary flow and increase strength. Silicon is a particularly good general purpose wire which strengthens brass and aids the capillary action on which the brazing technique relies. When working with cast iron, a manganese filler will produce good bonding; aluminum is used for joining or repairing

aluminum bronzes. Nickel will produce a high strength joint but it is very expensive and is generally only used to join stainless steel.

Unless you are working with aluminum, a general-purpose borax flux or a bronze brazing flux may be used for brazing. These are available as a paste, from a cone or in powder form for mixing with water.

Filler wires with solid flux coatings or with flux embedded in a serrated surface are also available.

Brazing requires a neutral flame. A blowtorch may be used for smaller items, but an oxy-acetylene torch is preferable. Joint surfaces must be perfectly clean; they must also be in very close contact to one another. The joint is prefluxed and then the parent metal is heated until the flux melts. When the filler wire is brought into contact with the joint, it should flow along and through the joint.

An advantage of brazing is that it can produce an almost invisible joint.

SUITABLE METALS
– brazing –

different metals
thin metal
aluminum
copper
brass
cast iron
mild steel
stainless steel

ALUMINUM BRAZING

Even though the term brazing implies the use of brass wire, it also encompasses capillary joints in general.

Aluminum may be brazed with an aluminum filler wire (silicon or silicon/copper) which will melt below the melting point of the pure metal – but a special flux for aluminum must be used.

The easiest gas joining process for aluminum is flame brazing, although considerable skill is required in maintaining the critical balance of heat input and temperature.

* Note that most metals may be brazed, including iron, mild steel, copper, brass, stainless steel, and aluminimum. Different types of metal may also be brazed to one another. However, when brazing, the different types of metal must be heated to the specific temperature required for that metal. For example, a considerably higher temperature will be required for stainless steel than for ordinary mild steel.

TOP LEFT
Mild steel must be cleaned using a flat metal file, sandpaper or steel wool.

BOTTOM LEFT
When the required temperature is reached, place the tip of the brazing rod on the joint and allow it to melt into the joint.

TOP RIGHT
Bronze brazing flux is used with a bronze brazing rod.

RIGHT
An oxy-acetylene torch is the preferred tool for brazing. Oxy-fuel equipment comprises oxygen, in the black cylinder (right), and acetylene in the shorter maroon cylinder.

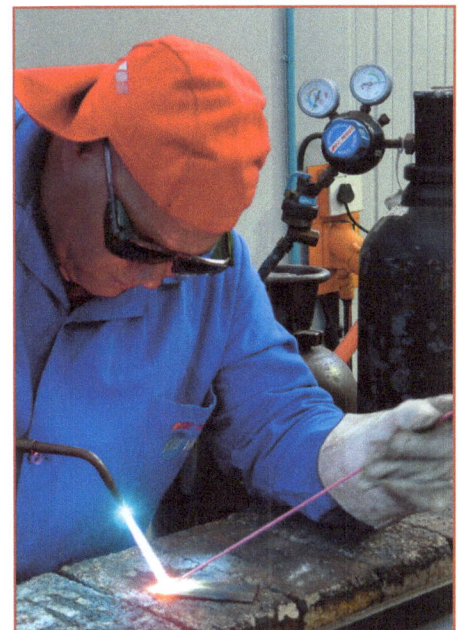

BRAZEWELDING

The name, brazewelding, is confusing, as the parent metal is not melted during the brazewelding process, so it is not a true fusion welding technique.

Also, the filler wires and fluxes used for brazewelding are the same as for brazing, which is a soldering technique.

Popular as a method of fabrication and for repair work, brazewelding produces very strong joints and is a much quicker process than fusion welding. As it is carried out at a much lower temperature than fusion welding, it results in less distortion. It also ensures total bonding between the parent metal and the high strength brass deposit of the filler material.

Brazewelding may be used on most metals that have a higher melting point than the brazewelding rod (850–900 degrees C/ 1562–1652 degrees F). The relatively low temperatures required are of particular advantage when working with cast iron and other malleable irons. When working with cast iron (which is quite brittle), it is still advisable to preheat the metal to be welded to minimize the risk of cracking.

It is a useful technique for joining different types of metals together as the brass-based filler effectively acts as a bridge between the metals. This filler is also beneficial when joining thin sections of metal to thicker sheets or where you need a smooth profile and do not want to grind the metal after you have welded it (for example when replacing car bodywork).

SUITABLE METALS
– brazewelding –

coated metals
different metals
thin metal
cast iron
galvanized iron
mild steel

Another advantage is that it is safer when working with coated metals. Ordinary fusion welding techniques burn off metal coatings and produce hazardous fumes.

Edge preparation is similar to that used for fusion welding. The metal surface should be cleaned at least 12 mm/ .472 in back from the joint seam on each side and all corners should be rounded off to reduce stress points and to provide an unbroken surface for good bonding.

Prefluxing is not important for braze-welding. In fact, since the flux is transmitted via the filler wire, the only really important preparation required is thorough cleaning and degreasing.

AWS A5.27R (sometimes called M15) Bronze is the recommended rod for all brazewelding applications – and it should be used in conjunction with AWS A5.27R Brazing Flux.

The end of the rod is heated and then dipped into the flux. When the wire touches the heated surface, the flux will transfer to its surface even before the wire melts. This part of the technique is also similar to fusion welding; the appearance of the brazeweld deposit is also the same, except that it is brass or bronze in color.

Flux coated rods are available and combine flux and brazing filler metal in a single convenient form.

When brazewelding, if the joint is not hot enough, 'wetting' will not occur. If it is too hot, the zinc oxide will tend to burn off in white fumes; these are toxic and should not be inhaled. Lack of oxygen in the flame will also result in a honey-combed, porous weld.

When the brazewelding process is complete, the residual flux must be brushed away from the surface

ABOVE
Safety apparel is essential when doing any of the work outlined in this book, including gloves and goggles. Note that a leather apron will prevent sparks from getting on to clothing and possibly setting it alight.

LEFT
Types of joints commonly used for brazewelding.

THICKNESS	JOINT TYPE			
	BUTT	LAP	TEE	ANGLE
Plate thicker than 5 mm/0.196 in				
Sheet thinner than 5 mm/0.196 in				
Tube and pipe 1 mm/0.39 in thick				
Sheet thinner than 1 mm/0.39 in				
Tube with a wall thinner than 1mm/0.39 in				

GAS WELDING

One of the earliest fusion welding techniques used, gas welding is ideal for welding tubes and small diameter pipe and is often used for repairs. It is well suited for use with mild steel, but may also be used with most other metals, provided they are not too thick.

Gas welding equipment is discussed in some detail on pages 11 and 12. Remember that it is safe provided it is used correctly and always in accordance with the manufacturer's instructions. Since leaking connections are a major cause of accidents, it is a good idea to keep a leak detection spray in the workshop and to use it before you start work.

Preparation is vital for a successful project. You will need the correct nozzle

ABOVE
A typical worker ready to do gas welding with the correct gauges and color coded pipes connected to the correct gas cylinders.

RIGHT
The thickness of the metal to be welded will determine how the edges are prepared.

SUITABLE METALS
– gas welding –

mild steel
aluminum
cast iron
stainless steel
wrought iron

---

for the job. This is determined by various factors including the type and thickness of the metal, and the joint you are making. Generally thicker metal requires more heat, so you will use a larger nozzle. However, if the nozzle is too big, it will produce an unstable flame which could cause a flashback. If a nozzle is too small, you will need more gas to produce sufficient heat to weld, and the resultant flame will be harsh.

You will need the correct welding rod for each project (see table below). You may also need flux, although mild steel is an exception.

EDGE PREPARATION

It is usually necessary to prepare the edges which are to be welded together, the exact process depending on the material and its thickness.

The thickness of the metal you are welding will help determine how it should be joined.

A plain square-edged butt joint can be made in thin steel if the edges are true and

clean. Thicker metal plate requires a V-shaped joint so that the flame and welding rod can penetrate the full depth of the join.

Flanged joints may be used for thin sheet steel, brass and copper, but not for aluminum or aluminum alloys. The edges of sheet metal up to 1,5 mm/ .059 in thick may be flanged in a machine or by bending in a vice or jig to a depth of about twice the thickness of the metal. However, a plain butt joint, suitably tacked or clamped is generally preferred.

For metal between 1,5 mm and 3,5 mm/ .059 in and .137 in, edges can be square, but they should be separated by a gap equal to half the thickness of the material. Thickish metal (3,5 mm–5 mm/ .137 in–.196 in) can be welded using the leftward technique (see page 26) providing edges are bevelled to the full depth to give a total angle of 80 degrees. Even thicker metal (5–8 mm/ .196 in–.314 in) can be welded without bevelled edges using the rightward technique (see page 26 and illustration below). Anything thicker than 8 mm/ .314 in requires the rightward technique and edges must be bevelled to a total 60 degree angle for the full depth of the material.

While it is possible to weld steel plate up to 16 mm/ .629 in in thickness using oxy-acetylene equipment, the process is slow and so it becomes expensive compared to electric welding. It is advisable to use electric equipment for any sheet metal thicker than 10 mm/ .393 in, unless you are welding narrow strip metal, flat bars and round metal.

THICKNESS OF METAL	DIAMETER OF ROD	EDGE PREPARATION FOR BUTT WELDS IN STEEL	
< 1 mm < 0.039 in	1.2–1.6 mm 0.047–0.062 in		
1–3.2 mm 0.393–0.125 in	1.6–3.2 mm 0.062–0.125 in		0.8–3.2 mm 0.031–0.125 in
3.2–5 mm 0.125–0.196 in	3.2–4 mm 0.125–0.157 in	80° V	0.8–3.2 mm 0.031–0.125 in
4.8–8 mm 0.188–0.314 in	3.2–4 mm 0.125–0.157 in		3.2–4 mm 0.125–0.157 in
8–16 mm 0.314–0.629 in	4–6.4 mm 0.157–0.251 in	60° V	0.8–3.2 mm 0.031–0.125 in
> 16 mm > 0.629 in	6.4 mm 0.251 in	top V 60° bottom V 80°	3.2–4 mm 0.125–0.157 in

WELDING METHODS

Gas welding is a relatively slow process which takes practise to perfect.

Good co-ordination is required to produce a neutral gas flame, control the molten weld pool, melt the parent metal and feed the welding rod (filler) all at the same time.

Valves control the release of the gas and oxygen required for the blowtorch, and it may take a little time to achieve the correct 'neutral' flame used for most welding work. Start by opening the valve of the blow pipe which controls the acetylene gas, just a little. Light the gas and then slowly turn on the oxygen. The flame will turn from a bright yellow/orange to blue, with a brilliant cone and bluish outer feather. A neutral flame has equal quantities of oxygen and acetylene and a very small cone (with no chemical reactions between it and the weld material). If you release too much acetylene, the flame will not be hot enough, and it will carbonize. If this happens, you will notice that the cone becomes quite pronounced. If there is too much oxygen, and not enough acetylene, the flame will be too hot.

It is also important to hold the torch correctly. The greater the angle it forms above the metal, the better the heat will penetrate. But if you are working with thin metal, you do not want this to happen, so you will need to use a shallow angle to reduce the risk of burn-through.

In some applications the rod and torch are moved forwards (or leftwards); in others, they are moved backwards (known as rightwards).

Leftward welding is used to make flanged edge welds on mild steel; for unbevelled edges up to 3,5 mm/ .137 in; and on bevelled edges which are 3,5–5 mm/ .137 in–.196 in thick. It is also used for welding cast iron and non-ferrous metals.

The metal thickness will determine how long it takes to produce a weld pool. Once the pool is about 4 mm/ .157 wide, and melting well, you can move the torch along the sheet, taking care to keep the width of the pool constant. If the pool spreads, move faster. If it seems to 'dry up', slow down to make sure the metal continues to melt.

Presuming you are right-handed, start welding on the righthand end of the joint and work leftwards. Move the torch forward with just enough side-to-side movement to ensure that both edges of the metal and the welding rod melt. It is important to keep the rod and the nozzle of the torch at the correct angle while you work (see illustrations right).

Rightward welding (sometimes called backhand welding) is only used for steel plates which are thicker than 5 mm/ .196 in. Edges between 5 mm and 8 mm/ .196 in and .314 in do not need to be bevelled, but anything thicker than 8 mm/ .314 in should be bevelled to a 60 degree angle.

The weld is started at the lefthand end of the joint and the torch is moved rightwards. Point the flame towards the metal being deposited so that heat is concentrated in the weld pool. Hold the rod at a right angle and move it round and round, keeping the flame centerd and steady to ensure even melting of the metal. Make sure the bottom corners of the join melt to form a circular shape.

GAS WELDED JOINTS

There are five basic weld joints: butt, corner, edge, lap and tee-joints. Corner and butt joints can be welded relatively quickly and they require less heat than lap joints or lap fillets.

It is often necessary to tack-weld components together before you start welding. This will enable you to assemble several pieces of metal at once and will keep the sections together while you weld. Tacks may be made longer and less frequently as the metal thickness increases.

Never put welded joints into water to cool them down otherwise the metal will become hard and brittle.

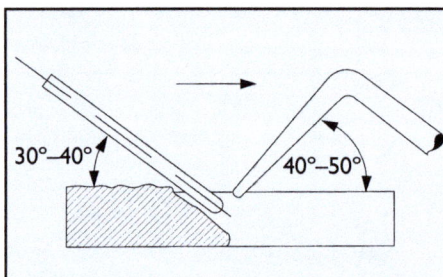

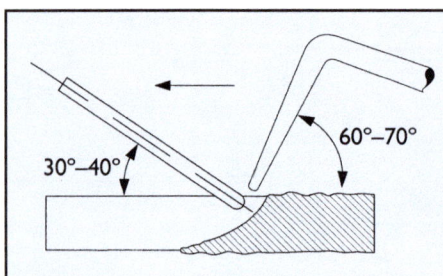

TOP LEFT
Rightward welding is executed from left to right, in a backwards (or backhand) motion. You can see from the drawing what angles the torch and welding rod should be held at to ensure a good joint.

BOTTOM LEFT
Leftward welding relies on the forward movement of both the torch and welding rod. Again, you can see from the illustration at what angles the torch and welding rod should be held to ensure a good joint.

TOP RIGHT
Gas welding takes practise to perfect, but once you get the hang of it you'll find it really isn't difficult. The first step is to get the flame right. Open the valve that controls the acetylene gas, just a little. Ignite the gas and then slowly turn on the oxygen. The flame will turn from a bright yellow-orange color to blue, with a brilliant cone and bluish outer 'feather'. It is essential that the flame setting is correct. If it isn't hot enough it will carbonize and the blue cone will be quite pronounced; if it is too hot, it will sound fierce.

RIGHT
A neutral flame has equal quantities of oxygen and acetylene.

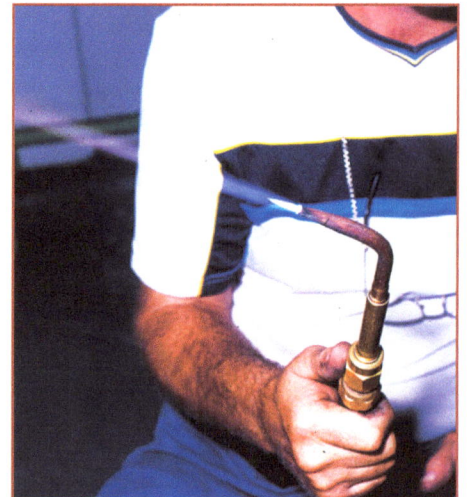

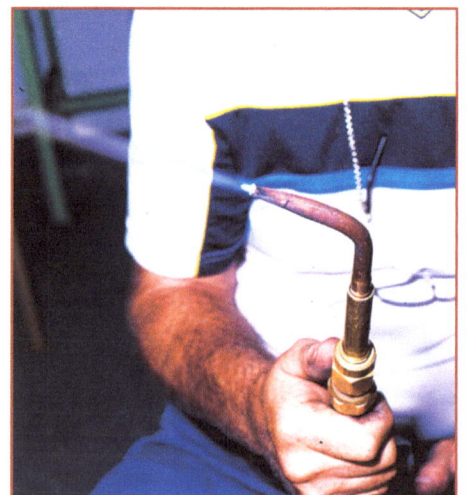

MMA WELDING

The manual metal arc (MMA) process relies on electricity to produce heat for welding, and it is the most common welding method used by DIY metalworkers.

The way it works is that an electric arc is struck between the metal being welded and a flux-coated filler wire (the electrode). In essence, the extreme heat of the arc melts the electrode and the metal, which then mix together to form the weld.

It is not difficult to weld different thicknesses of metal using the MMA method, and welding different types of metal together is also not a problem, as long as the correct electrodes are used.

During the arc welding process, the heat (which can be as high as 4000 degrees C/ 7232 degrees F) is controlled by the current setting and the size of the electrode, which must be compatible with the current used. If the current is increased and the arc becomes erratic, it is generally sufficient to use a larger electrode to accommodate the electrical current. Excessive current will also result in overheating of the electrode which will cause defects in the weld and usually a rough, spattered surface.

Like gas welding, MMA welding is perfectly safe, provided the equipment is used correctly and safeguards are put into place. For instance it is essential to use the correct personal protective clothing (PPC)

and gear. Above all, it is vital to wear a helmet with filter glass to protect your eyes from the bright electric arc. If you do not, you could end up with arc eye, a condition caused by rays from the welding coming into contact with the eyes – even for a split second.

While arc eye does not normally cause permanent damage, your eyes will feel gritty and will probably be ultra-sensitive to light for several days afterwards.

Also, electricity is potentially lethal, so it is essential to ensure that the workbench and metal you are working on are properly earthed. If you are working on a metal workbench, earth to the bench; if you are using a metal vice on a wooden bench, earth to the vice.

You must also ensure that the welding lead is connected to the terminal marked 'electrode', and that the work lead is connected to the terminal marked 'work'. These are basic rules that must always be followed.

WELDING METHOD

These instructions form the basics that you need to master to weld using MMA equipment.

To start the arc, scrape the end of the electrode across the parent metal so that current starts to flow through the circuit. Then raise the electrode about 4 mm/ .157 in above the surface of the metal, allowing the current to flow across the gap and create the arc.

With practise, you will soon establish the optimum length of an arc. A good rule of thumb is to keep it as short as possible, although if it is too short, the electrode may stick and leave rough deposits of slag (or slag inclusions) on the surface. If the arc is too long, penetration of the metal will be reduced and the molten electrode will spatter, resulting in a weld with a rough finish.

When joining two pieces of metal together, it is essential to produce a smooth weld bead. To achieve this, hold the electrode at a 60 degree angle and move it slowly along the joint, keeping the bead uniform and regular.

On thicker sections, several runs may be required. To form a neat weld, make these in single runs.

SUITABLE METALS
– MMA welding –

mild steel
aluminum
carbon steel (all types)
cast iron
copper
stainless steel
wrought iron

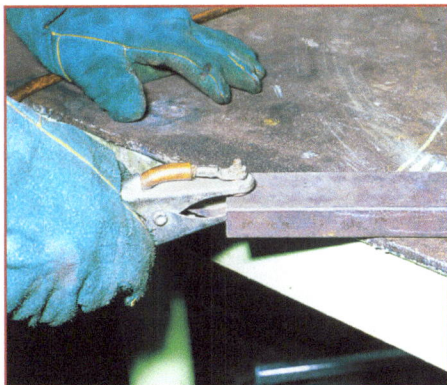

ABOVE LEFT
Before you start welding, make sure that the metal is clean and free from rust or any oily residue. Then choose the correct electrode for the metal and for the job, check the root gap, and set the welding current. Now you can clamp the earth to the metal you are going to weld.

ABOVE RIGHT
Position the electrode and switch on the MMA machine.

BELOW LEFT
When you have completed the weld, alalow the flux to cool, and then use a metal weld hammer to chip off tany slag that has formed.

BELOW RIGHT
Use a wire brush to cean the joint.

To finish off a bead, weld to the end of the joint and fill in at the end of the weld for a couple of seconds; then weld back in the opposite direction for about 5 mm/ .196 in without changing the angle of the rod. This will fill any gaps at the end of the weld and prevent cracking when it cools.

The angle of the electrode and its 'travel speed' (the speed at which you move it along the joint) are both important. Correct travel speed for normal welding applications varies between 125 and 375 mm/ 4.921 in and 1 ft 2.763 in per minute. If you move it too fast, penetration and fusion will both be poor. If it is moved too slowly, you will produce a defective weld, possibly with slag inclusions (where solid materials are trapped in the solidifying metal) and overlapping of the weld.

As you work, the electrode will melt away. When only about 50 mm/ 1.968 in is left, you must replace it. Once the weld is complete, the slag must be chipped off the surface. It is easier and safer to remove once it has cooled. Finally, clean the join with a wire brush.

Tacks. When working with sheets of metal, it is good practise to clamp pieces together and then tack the metal together before welding.

Tacks should be at least 6 mm/ .236 in long and they should be longer but less frequent the thicker the metal.

Fillet Welding. Fillets are the most common MMA welding joints. They generally form lap, tee and corner joints with the weld placed in a corner, without any gap, and in a more or less triangular shape.

Preparation for fillet joints is minimal, since the weld does not need to penetrate the full thickness of the metal. However, it is important that the metal you are welding is clean, close fitting, and that all the edges you are welding are square. On sheared plate, it is advisable to remove 'false cuts'.

Fillet joints are used for T-joints, lap joints and corner joints:

☆ T-joints

The weld metal should fuse into, or penetrate the corner formed between the two pieces of metal. Ideally, it should form a natural V-shaped fillet.

☆ Lap joints

These are often used in arc welding to 'thicken up' the material. For full strength, fill the joint to the top of the edge of the lap but melt the edge as little as possible so that it has a smooth finish.

☆ Corner joints

These joints have a V-shaped groove in which a fillet weld is deposited. Fusion should be complete for the full thickness of the metal. It is often necessary to have a gap or a slight overlap on the corner.

Butt welding. Not as common as fillet welding (and more difficult to execute accurately), butt welds will enable you to join two pieces of metal up against each other. Unlike a butt joint made with wood, there are several configurations which may be used. These depend largely on the thickness of the metal you are working with.

The first run in any butt weld should be deposited with an electrode no bigger than 4 mm/ .157 in, maintaining an angle of 70–85 degrees. The root gap (which is the space between the prepared edges – or root faces – that have not been bevelled) must be maintained by tacking, otherwise it will tend to close during welding.

☆ Square butt weld

No need to prepare edges, which should be separated slightly to allow fusion through the full thickness of the steel. Can be used with plate up to 6 mm/ .236 in thick.

☆ Single V-butt weld

Commonly used for plate up to 16 mm/ .629 in thick, and for even thicker metal where access is from one side only. If welding from one side only, use a backing bar to ensure complete fusion.

☆ Double V-butt weld

Allows faster welding and greater economy of electrodes when used with 12 mm/ .472 in and thicker plate, and when welding from both sides. Will also distort less.

☆ Single U-butt weld

Best suited for metal thicker than 40 mm/ 1.574 in, although preparation is more expensive as the metal must be machined. Quicker when used on thick plates rather than a single V; also less contraction and less tendency to distort.

☆ Double U-butt weld

Used on thick plate that is accessible for welding from both sides.

☆ Horizontal butt weld

The lower piece of metal must be bevelled to about 16 degrees and the upper piece to 45 degrees, resulting in a total (or included) angle of 60 degrees. This provides a ledge on the lower piece of metal which will tend to retain the metal as it melts during the welding process.

ABOVE
A well executed fillet weld forming a neat and even triangle shape between the two pieces of metal.

LEFT
The most popular butt joints that are produced by arc welding.

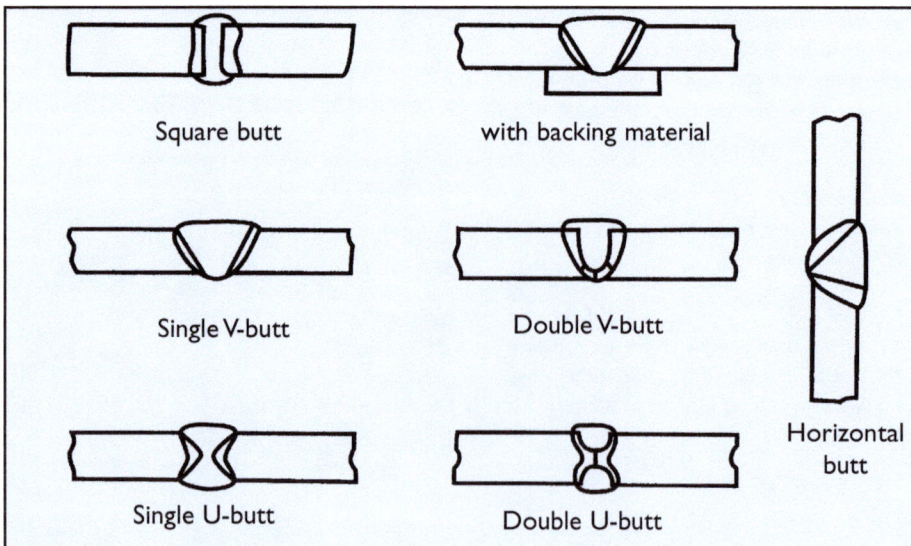

Square butt | with backing material

Single V-butt | Double V-butt

Single U-butt | Double U-butt | Horizontal butt

MIG WELDING

A process that involves gas shielding of the arc with either inert or active gases, metal inert gas (MIG) welding is a technique that has several other names. For instance, it is also known as metal active gas (MAG), because of the chemical reaction between the shielding gas (CO_2) and the weld metal. And for the same reason it is also often referred to as CO_2 welding. However, the term more frequently used in the United States and in welding engineering circles internationally is gas metal arc welding (GMAW).

MIG welding or GMAW is a much cleaner process than manual metal arc welding. Instead of electrodes, filler wire is housed in a roll in the machine or in a separate unit, and fed continuously to the arc, where it melts and becomes part of the weld metal. A shielding gas is also fed to the weld area to protect the weld metal. Only minor weld spatter is produced during the process and, since a flux is not used, slag doesn't form and get trapped in the weld.

Although the actual welding process is simple, and in fact follows the same basic procedures as MMA welding (see pages 27–28), the set-up of a MIG welding machine is fairly complex and requires a good understanding of the parameters involved. These relate to the voltage of the

SUITABLE METALS
– MIG welding –

aluminum
carbon steels
cast iron
stainless steel
wrought iron

---

arc, the wire feed speed and inductance, which determines the rate the current rises through the wire, and it must be properly balanced.

It is also essential that a stable arc is produced; that the correct amount of weld metal is used; and the right heat is applied for adequate fusion. If the procedure is not correctly followed, the metal simply will not weld properly.

The amperage of the MIG machine is adjusted according to the thickness of the metal being welded. Generally, thin metal requires a low amperage and low wire feed, while thick metal requires a high amperage and high wire feed.

Different types of wire spools are available for the full range of materials including carbon steels, stainless steel, aluminum and its alloys, and nickel alloys. The wire is fed through the torch, which has a copper tip made to suit the diameter of the wire. It is heated at the point of contact.

JOINTS

Much of the skill in making good joints relates to settings on the machine. Welding requires constant assessment of the shape and size of the weld pool and immediate corrective action must be taken when necessary,

Tacking is usually easier using a MIG machine than with a manual metal arc welder or gas welding machine. The wire touches the point at which the tack is required and all you need to do is press the switch. Even though an MMA tack is instant, if you do not get it right first time, you may leave unwanted 'flashes' on the surface.

LEFT ABOVE
Position the MIG torch and pull the trigger to feed the wire.

LEFT BELOW
As the wire strikes the joint, the welding arc is established under a shroud of shielding gas to weld the parts together.

Butt joints can be made easily with sheet metal from 1 mm to 3 mm/ .039 in to .118 in thick, using a single pass with a gap of 0.75 mm/ .029 in x the thickness of the metal, and requires no edge preparation. For plate butts, a 60 degree V is used with a root face and root gap of 1.5 mm/ .059 in.

TIG WELDING

The most difficult manual arc welding process to master, TIG welding involves more expensive equipment and it is also a relatively slow process when compared to MMA and even MIG welding. However it is possible to produce the very best quality welds which is why it is used primarily in industrial situations, especially those industries working with high-quality metal sheet and pipes made from stainless steel and aluminum alloys, rather than for DIY projects. It is the only manual option if X-ray quality welds are required.

Like MIG welding, TIG welding has several different names: tungsten inert gas (TIG), argon arc welding and the more formal one, gas tungsten arc welding (GTAW).

Primarily a specialist process, TIG welding falls within a category of 'non-consumable' arc welding techniques.

Instead of using a 'consumable' electrode, (that is literally used up during the welding process) filler wire is used in the same way as in gas welding. During this welding process, an arc is formed between the metalwork and a tungsten electrode, but the electrode does not melt.

TIG welding, like MIG welding, relies on shielding gases, but unlike the MIG (or GMAW process) only inert gases that don't react or combine with other gases are used.

While co-ordination of the arc and filler material is difficult and it takes experience and expertise to master this technique, one of its biggest advantages is that it can be used to weld a wide range of different metals and metal alloys that cannot be successfully welded using other arc welding processes.

SUITABLE METALS
– TIG welding –

aluminum
nickel
caron and stainless steel
titanium
magnesium
brass and bronze
gold

TROUBLESHOOTING: WELD DEFECTS

Defect type	Illustration	Description	Cause
Longitudinal and transverse cracks in the craters, throat, toe, root, underbead and heat affected zone (HAZ) of the weld.	longitudinal · transverse · toe · HAZ · underbead · face · root · underbead · crater	Cracks which are characterized by sharp tips and a high length to width ratio.	Improper termination of the weld; fast cooling rates; highly restrained joints; low ductility of weld metal; shrinkage stresses; weld beads too small; presence of hydrogen picked up in the weld metal from moist electrodes and oil on the plate.
Porosity in the weld bead.	weld bead porosity · surface porosity	Cavities or holes scattered in the weld bead or on its surface. Holes are generally round or elongated.	Trapped gas from welding process; contamination during welding from oil, paint or coatings on the plate; incorrect welding current or arc length; incompatible filler material.
Slag inclusions.	slag inclusions	Non-metallic inclusions of slag and oxides trapped in the solidifying metal.	Incorrect welding techniques; improper cleaning of the weld between passes; sharp notches in the joint faces; lack of adequate access to the joint for welding.
Incomplete fusion between plate and weld metal.	face · face · adjacent weld bead	Failure of liquid weld metal to fuse into the faces of the joint or to adjacent weld beads.	Incorrect welding techniques; not enough heat in the joint; improper joint design; oxidized joint faces; lack of access to joint faces.
Incomplete penetration of the weld through the joint.	root opening or gap · root face · root	Weld does not penetrate through full thickness of the joint.	Root face too thick; root opening too small; electrode diameter too large for the root opening; welding current too low; improper control of the electrode.
Underfill.	weld surface	Surface of the weld bead (or part of it) lies below the surface of the base material.	Weld joint not completely filled.
Overlap.	joint edges	Unfused weld metal protrudes beyond the edges of the joint forming an undesirable notch.	Travel speed too slow; incorrect preparation of joint.
Undercut.	grooves in plate	A groove in the plate adjacent to the weld bead which has been left unfilled.	Welding current too high, travel speed too high; too large an electrode-to-work angle.

3
FINISHING METHODS

FINISHING METHODS

All metal requires some kind of finishing coat or protective film to prevent it from corrosion. Ferrous metals, in particular, are prone to rusting and should be galvanized, plated or painted. Even though some non-ferrous metals (particularly copper, zinc and aluminum) automatically develop a protective film of oxide which will prevent corrosion, the appearance of some objects and items will be improved if they are polished, painted or given some kind of decorative finish.

Tools and hardware that cannot be painted can be smeared with grease or sprayed with a proprietary oil to prevent them from rusting.

CLEANING

Whatever finish you decide to give metal objects, they must be clean and degreased before you start.

Rough welds and spatter must be dressed (neatened) and cleaned. You can use an angle grinder on flat weld areas, and a small rotary grinding tool will get into corners. Initial preparation is often done by simply filing to remove rough edges or by wire brushing. If you use a disc sander, great care must be taken not to remove too much of the material as this could alter its shape.

Where reactive fluxes have been used for soldering, these must be removed before any type of finishing coat is applied. If a soldered joint is to be painted, or if the finish is untidy, you may need to remove excess passive flux as well. This is usually done using an organic solvent or with hot, soapy water and a wire brush.

Most metals can also be rubbed down with a fairly coarse, abrasive emery cloth. Then use a fine-grade emery cloth which has been lubricated with a little mineral oil or motor oil to get it perfectly smooth.

Most metals can be swabbed in mineral turpentine to remove grease prior to painting. Steel can be successfully degreased by washing it in a caustic soda solution. You can make this at home by mixing 200 g/ 7.05 oz caustic soda with about four litres of water, adding a couple of squirts of washing up liquid to the mixture. Heat until it starts to simmer and the caustic soda is completely dissolved.

Aluminum can be degreased in a solution of 75 g/ 2.64 oz washing soda and four litres of water, also heated on the stove.

Hydrochloric acid and hot water also works well.

Whatever method you use for cleaning, be sure to rinse the metalwork in fresh water afterwards.

POLISHING

Buffing and polishing non-ferrous metals like copper, brass and silver will produce a bright metallic finish which is usually preferred for decorative items.

Use a wet pumice stone or pumice powder to remove any scratches before you buff or polish the metal. To buff it, use a polishing attachment on your electric drill (see page 9) with buffing 'soap' or polishing compound. This 'soap' (or polish) comes in various grades, fine, medium and coarse, and will enable you to remove any minor scratches and discoloration. Even though

the metal gets hot during the buffing process, do not wear gloves as they can get caught. Be sure to wear safety glasses.

Once metal has been buffed, a proprietary metal polish can be used to create lustre. Some polishes are made with materials that will retard oxidization.

To avoid the need for frequent polishing, you can apply a lacquer finishing coat. Professional companies usually dip items in lacquer to produce an even, unmarked finish. It can also be brushed or sprayed onto the surface.

COATINGS

Various processes are used to give metal an extra protective skin. Methods include powder coating, electro-galvanizing (with silver) and hot-dip galvanizing (see page 33). Metal items may also be plated with another metal to improve their surface finish. Silver and brass plating is often used to coat decorative bowls, jugs and so on. Zinc plating, achieved in a process known as sharadizing, gives a high degree of protection.

All these processes require specialised machinery and equipment and should be outsourced once your project is complete. If you are planning to make several items, it will be more cost-effective to send them off in a batch for finishing.

POWDER COATING
Commonly referred to as epoxy coating, this finishing method involves several processes. First the item is washed in an acid bath to thoroughly clean and degrease it. It is then rinsed and allowed to dry. The powder coating, available in a range of colors, is sprayed onto the metal before it is baked in a special oven at high temperature.

PREVIOUS PAGE
A huge bundle of metal items is raised from the 'bath' where it has been dipped into bubbling, molten metal for galvanising.

TOP RIGHT
A professional spray-gun used with compressed air.

ABOVE
A large variety of spray paints and colors are available in aerosol cans, which is ideal for small jobs.

GALVANIZING

Hot dip galvanizing provides a corrosion resistant coating on iron and steel and is commonly used to protect gates, fences and even outdoor furniture.

The color and texture of the galvanized metal varies quite radically, from a bright, sparkly finish to matt grey where the coating is converted to an iron-zinc alloy, depending exactly how the process is carried out.

Generally, the process involves cleaning the steel surface thoroughly in a controlled atmosphere before dipping the metal into molten zinc heated to about 450 degrees C/ 842 F for a few seconds. It is then passed through an aqueous solution to apply a chromate coating.

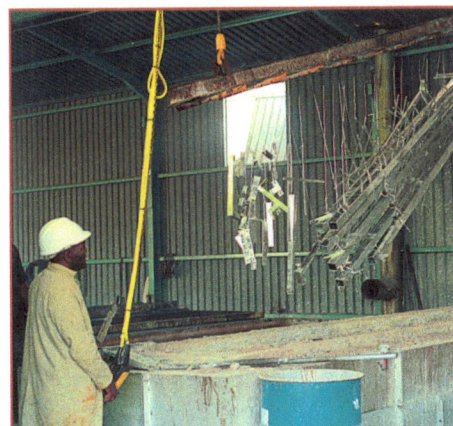

The subsequent resistance of galvanized metal to corrosion depends on the amount of zinc used and its thickness – a factor which is controlled by gas jets.

The metal can be galvanized before or after welding. If it has already been welded, it is vital that all welds are free from porosity as pores can trap acid which tends to escape after galvanizing, producing a rusty stain.

When MIG welding galvanized steel, there tends to be more spatter. This not only looks ugly, but it can also clog the welding gun and affect both the flow of the shielding gas and the feed of the wire. A spatter release compound reduces these problems.

A much higher heat input is needed to remove zinc from the weld pool when you are welding galvanized steel with an MMA machine. You will also need a lower welding speed to burn off as much of the zinc coating in front of the weld pool as possible.

ABOVE
When metal items are to be powder coated, they must first be degreased and then acid washed and rinsed before the powder coating can be applied.

ABOVE LEFT
Powder coating (or a type of epoxy) is sprayed onto metal in an isolated spray booth so that dust and dirt doesn't adhere to metal during the coating process.

CENTER LEFT
It is essential for operators to wear masks as they might otherwise enhale the fumes.

BELOW RIGHT
Galvanising is a finishing method which should be left to the professionals. Metal is dipped into a steaming bath and then lifted out again to cool and dry.

PAINT

Painting is the simplest finishing technique available, and it offers a remarkably wide variety of options they may be applied by hand or sprayed onto the surface.

Even though the preparation and painting of different metal surfaces may differ slightly (and they do), there are some golden rules that must be followed, irresepctive of what you are painting. These 'rules' relate largely to cleaning and preparation of the surface, as any contamination can affect the adhesion and drying of whatever paint is used. It is also essential to use the correct primer for the job.

Although most metals may be painted, brass, copper and lead are best left unpainted as these surfaces do not provide a 'key' for adhesion of the paint.

PREPARATION

Oil and grease must be removed before painting, preferably with a water soluble detergent or degreaser. Generally it is best to avoid organic solvents. Galvanized steel should be cleaned with a proprietary iron cleaner and rinsed with clean water.

Rust may be removed by wire brushing, chipping and/or sanding, or with a chemical rust remover. If chemicals are used, it is essential to clean these off thoroughly before painting.

Really bad rust and millscale (a hard, brittle oxide layer with a typical glossy blue-black surface) can be removed by abrasive blast cleaning, but the metal must be degreased first as oil and grease will contaminate the grit used for cleaning.

All welds must also be free from slag, slag inclusions and pinholes, and weld spatter must be removed from adjacent areas by grinding or scraping.

PRIMING

Metal should be primed as soon as it has been cleaned. Even a few hours exposure in a damp or polluted atmosphere can affect the performance of paint coatings. Moisture on bare metal can impair adhesion of the primer, so it must be allowed to dry thoroughly before painting.

There are various types of primers, such as ordinary metal primer which is manufactured for use on iron and steel; water-based primer designed for use on galvanized steel, but also suitable for other surfaces such as mild steel; and etch primer, which is also suitable for galvanized steel.

When painting galvanized steel, it is important to use a primer that is compatible with both the zinc used for galvanizing and the paint chosen.

PAINT TYPES

Most paints can be used for metal, providing the correct primer has been used. Always follow the manufacturer's instructions regarding the recommended application, including the primer required.

A good quality etch coat may be used without priming.

METHOD

Even though painting may be regarded as the simplest finishing technique, it is not always easy to get rid of the marks left by brush strokes. Spray painting, either with an aerosol can with or a spray gun, will often achieve a more professional finish.

SPECIAL EFFECTS

The more artistic handyman - or woman - can achieve a myriad of effects using paint and/or various solutions that will make the metal change color. The key here is to experiment using recipes and ideas provided by other people.

For instance, you will that by rubbing heated metal with a woollen cloth the cloth will be scorched. But if you continue rubbing the metal, the scorch will change the color of the metal.

Also, by heating ferrous metals and dipping them in mineral oil you can achieve an interesting blue-black finish. Alternatively, coat the metal with oil and then heat with a blowtorch to see what effects you can create.

Rust effect. Rust, which is created by a combination of water and oxygen, attacks iron and steel, causing it to deteriorate rapidly. While it is important to prevent corrosion, the weathered effect of rust has become a popular look for casual garden furniture. There are two ways that you can create a rust effect: with paint or by allowing the item to begin rusting naturally and to then thoroughly lacquer the surface to protect it from further decay.

Verdigris effect. Oxidization eventually causes brass and copper to discolor over time. But a nice soft green patina can be produced on brass and copper quite rapidly by brushing a mixture of vinegar, salt and sugar onto the surface of the metal for three or four days. A successful mixture may be made by dissolving a teaspoon of salt and tablespoon of fine sugar in about 100 ml/ 3.381 fl oz of vinegar.

Alternatively you can use paint to achieve a similar look. By using whiting or plaster of Paris powder over the wet paint, you can create an authentic crumbly effect

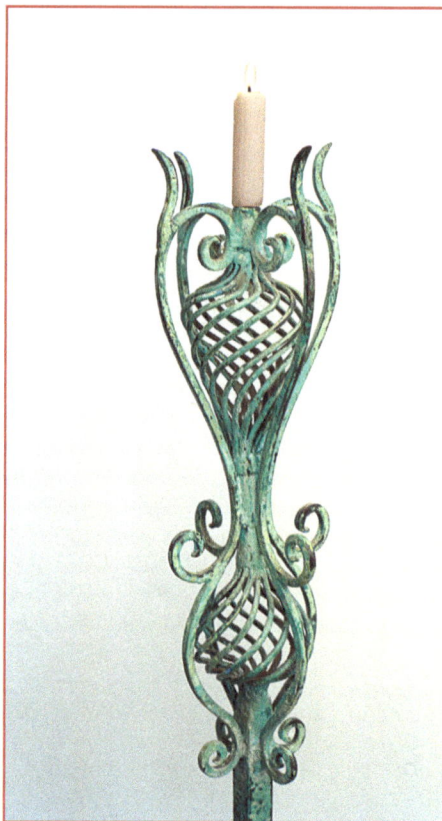

on the surface. Painted verdigris is surprisingly easy, and is a popular technique for metal objects, although it can be a little messy.

Start by spraying the primed metal with gold or copper paint. It will dry quickly; then brush on blue-green acrylic paint. Mix

ABOVE
An elaborate candle stick has been given a painted verdigris finish. A little gold paint smeered on the edges adds a little glitz and glamor.

ABOVE RIGHT
An unusual lampstand is painted with acrylic gold paint as a base to a verdigris finish.

CENTER RIGHT
A metal bench has been painted and sponged with color to make it appear as though it is rusted. A coat of clear sealer ensures that real rust doesn't set in.

BOTTOM RIGHT
Self-priming etch coat is a quick, easy and serviceable finish for practical items, like this fire screen made with diamond mesh and flat bar (see page 57).

a little all-purpose adhesive filler together with a little methylated spirits and turquoise- and aquamarine-hued acrylic paints to make two different colored pastes. They should have the consistency of soft butter icing. Paint the paste onto the metal randomly. Before it dries, sponge a little ochre paint into the paste. Then pour water over the whole object. While it is still wet, sprinkle whiting over the surface and press some of it into the paint and paste, particularly into recesses and moulded areas. When it has dried partially, wipe away some of the paint and paste to expose the metallic color underneath.

Allow to dry thoroughly before coating with an acrylic sealer.

4
PROJECTS

PROJECTS

The projects featured in this chapter range from very simple to reasonably challenging, and are suitable for beginners as well as those enthusiasts who have already developed basic metalworking skills.

All the items can be made with mild steel, which is easily accessible and reasonably straightforward to work with. A materials list accompanies each project, leaving you in no doubt as to what is required.

The tools and equipment you will need are also detailed, with suitable alternatives suggested wherever possible. The weekend welder will certainly not have all the equipment professional welders and metal-workers use; in some instances you may want to hire equipment or get someone else to do part of the job. Bear in mind that even some fulltime welders outsource cutting and bending, and many send their work to professional galvanizing and/or powder coating specialists for finishing.

You can, of course, tackle projects with other tools, and use different techniques to those specified. For instance, where an MMA machine is used, you may prefer to use a MIG welder, and vice versa. If you have access to oxy-acetylene equipment, you may prefer to gas weld. It really does not matter, provided you are confident using that particular technique.

Finishing procedures may also be altered, depending on preference.

The projects featured have been chosen for variety, and to give readers a selection of options that range in complexity. Several of the projects may also be easily adapted to produce different designs using the given elements.

For instance, the burglar bars illustrated on pages 52 and 53 can be easily reworked to create gates and fences. The balustrade idea shown on page 51 can also be used for gates and garden fences, as well as for burglar bars. The gate design on page 50, could just as easily be used for fencing, balustrades, or even to make very unusual burglar bars.

ABOVE
An attractive and unusual swimming pool fence made using the same design as that used for the gate on page 50.

LEFT
For safety reasons, it is essential to wear the correct gear when working on projects. A welding helmet with a correctly shaded lens will protect your eyes from the arc; gloves will protect your skin from possible burns.

RIGHT
A garden gate made with round mild steel bar and off-the-shelf spears follows the same design principles as the burglar bars featured on pages 52 and 53.

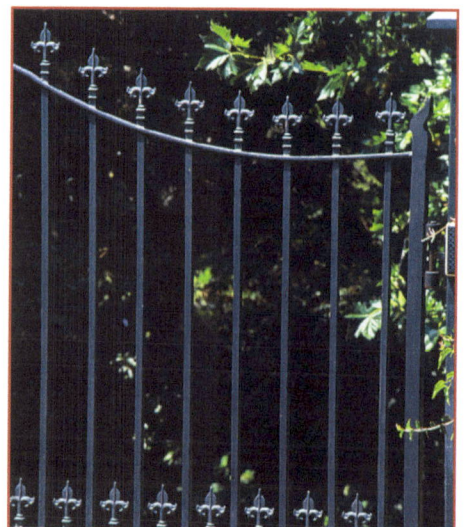

mm/ .062 in thick mild steel used to form the scoop, tongs and scraper ends.

Although the hanging rack is not included as a project, it is made with the same metal materials and tools specified below. Techniques simply involve bending two lengths of round bar to form the

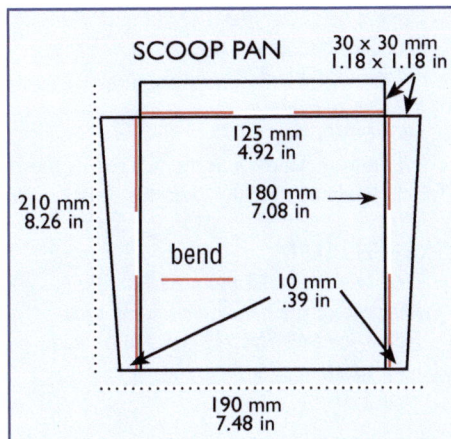

```
SCOOP PAN        30 x 30 mm
                 1.18 x 1.18 in
                 125 mm
                 4.92 in
210 mm           180 mm
8.26 in          7.08 in
    bend
                 10 mm
                 .39 in
        190 mm
        7.48 in
```

decorative top and welding this, and a few hooks, to a piece of flat mild steel.

To make these items, you will need a small welding machine with suitable electrodes; an MMA machine running at 50–80 amps is perfect, and it is unlikely that you will use more than one welding rod for the whole lot.

You will also need a retractable tape measure; a hacksaw; a bench-mounted vice; a piece of pipe with an inside diameter of 10–12 mm/ .393–.472 in to assist with bending; an angle grinder fitted with a grinding disc; a ball peen hammer to knock the bar into shape, as well as a chipping hammer to remove all residual slag after welding; and a paintbrush. Although jigs are not essential for these projects, you will find that a jig will be an invaluable tool to hold the handles in place while you weld on the various tops (see next page). A good jig is worth many pairs of helping hands!

If this is your first welding project, ask an engineering works to cut the flat metal to size for you according to the diagram, left.

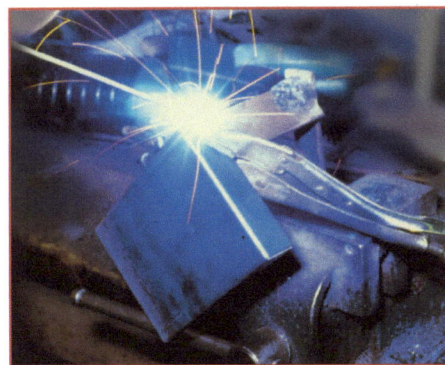

FIRE ACCESSORIES: SCOOP

An ideal series of projects for beginners, these accessories are perfect for use when barbecueng outdoors or burning winter fires indoors. All are made with 8 mm/ .314 in mild steel round bar handles with 1,6

CENTER LEFT

The flat piece of metal needs to be cut and bent according to the measurements shown in the diagram, left. You can use the techniques outlined on pages 18–21 or ask an engineering works to cut and bend the metal for you according to your neds.

RIGHT

The shape of the scoop makes it too awkward to secure in a vice. Instead, fix a piece of angle iron in the vice and clamp the scoop pan to the angle iron. Weld the corners of the two 30 mm x 30 mm/ 1.81 in x 1.81 closed.

BOTTOM LEFT

With the metal bar secured in a bench-mounted vice, measure and mark it at 170 mm/ 6.692 in from one end. Use a hacksaw to do this, but only scratch the surface; do not cut through the metal. This is the point where you will bend the top of the handle of the scoop.

BOTTOM RIGHT

Move the bar so that the mark you have just made is flush with the end of the vice. Slot the pipe onto the end of the bar and cold bend it back towards the vice.

ABOVE LEFT
Use the ball peen hammer to knock the bent end towards the rest of the bar. This will form the handle of the scoop.

ABOVE RIGHT
Put the new handle into the vice grip and weld the bent end back onto the shaft.

CENTER LEFT
Bend over about 15 mm/ .590 in of the other end of the handle and hammer it against the bar. This will give you a much more substantial surface to weld onto the scoop pan.

CENTER RIGHT
Now you can spot weld the handle to the pan. A homemade jig holds the pan and handle of the scoop together during welding.

BELOW
Weld the handle to the scoop pan.

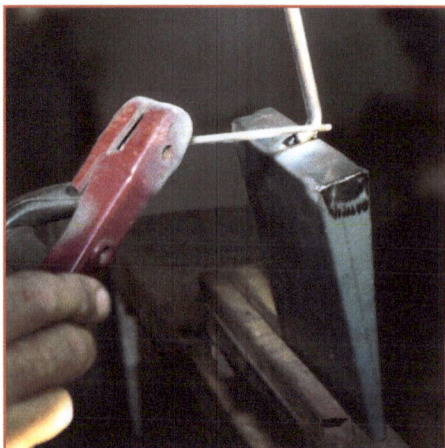

LEFT
Remove the scoop from the jig and secure in the vice. Now that it has been spot welded, you can work with it in an upright position.

RIGHT
Paint every exposed piece of metal with etch primer. Start at the edges and then paint inwards. Only one coat of this quick-drying self-priming paint is required.

FIRE ACCESSORIES: SCRAPER

This coal scraper, ideal for your fireplace or barbecue, is made exactly the same way as the scoop, except that the handle is slightly longer.

Follow the steps shown on the two previous pages and then weld the scraper instead of the scoop pan to the handle.

FIRE ACCESSORIES: TONGS

These tongs, shown hanging on the lefthand side of the fire accessories rack on page 37 is a useful tool for any type of fireplace or barbecue where wood or coal is burned.

The most complicated part of this project is bending the handle accurately.

To do this you need to make a jig with a piece of pipe or some other scrap of metal which is about 50 mm/ 1.968 in diameter. Alternatively clamp a piece of pipe this same diameter in the vice.

MATERIALS
– coal scraper –

Mild steel round bar:
  850 mm/ 2 ft 9.464 in [8 mm/ .314 in]
Mild steel flat sheet:
  100 mm x 25 mm/ 3.937 in x .984 in
  [3 mm/ .118 in]

MATERIALS
– coal tongs –

Mild steel round bar:
  1,5 m/ 4 ft 11.055 in [8 mm/ .314 in]
Mild steel flat sheet:
  2 x 65 mm x 50 mm/ 2 x 2.559 in x 1.968 in
  [1,6 mm/ .062 in]

ABOVE LEFT
The handle of the coal scraper is made exactly the same way as the handle of the scoop.

ABOVE RIGHT
Weld the rectangular metal piece to the bar.

ABOVE CENTER LEFT
Chip off all the slag using a metal chipping hammer.

ABOVE CENTER RIGHT
Clean well and paint with etch primer.

CENTER LEFT
The tongs are made by bending the bar to create a ring in the center at the top. Two 65 mm x 50 mm/ 2.559 x 1.968 plates are then welded to the two ends. To improve the grip, the bottom 15 mm/ .590 in must be bent at an angle of approximately 30 degrees. You can do this yourself by securing 15 mm/ .590 in in the vice and then cold bending it by hand.

CENTER RIGHT
Use a jig to bend the bar in the middle.

BELOW LEFT AND RIGHT
Secure the bar in the vice and position the tong ends under the bar, in the center, with the bent end at the base, then weld the bar to the flat metal.

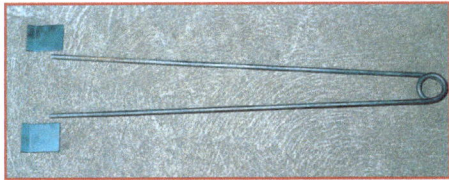

MATERIALS
– drinks holder –

Mild steel round bar:
  850 mm/ 2 ft 9.464 in [8 mm/ .314 in]
  925 mm/3 ft .417 in [6 mm/ .236 in]
Plastic ferrules:
  6 [6 mm/ .236 in]

DRINKS HOLDER

An ingenious portable stand designed to hold wine glasses and tumblers can be made in just a couple of hours. One end is cut to an angle so it can be pushed into the soil anywhere in the garden or on the beach.

To make the drinks stand you will need a welding machine (an MMA machine running at 50–80 amps is ideal) with suitable electrodes. One 2.50 mm/ .098 in welding rod was used for this project.

You will also need a bench mounted vice; a hacksaw, bandsaw or an angle grinder fitted with a 1 mm/ .039 in-thick disc, as well as files to finish off. Jigs are indispensable tools, both to shape and support the metal. These are easily made from found objects or by welding various offcuts together. The secret is to be innovative. For instance, a piece of pipe welded to a piece of flat metal can be used to make curves.

ABOVE LEFT
Round metal bar (6 mm/ .236 in and 8 mm/ .314 in) is used to make the drinks holder; and you will need plastic ferrules for the open ends. In addition, you will need at least two jigs for the project; one to bend the bar at an angle and the other to make the rings. You can use scrap metal and weld pieces together to form the jigs. The ingenious round jig shown here is in fact the discarded front hub of an old four wheel drive truck! Before you start, cut the 6 mm/ .236 in bar so that you have 2 x 80 mm/ 3.149 in pieces and 2 x 150 mm/ 5.905 in lengths bent to form a 90 degree angle.

CENTER LEFT
To make the rings, wind what is left of the 6 mm/ .236 in bar around the circular jig. This ingenious turning jig is rotated using a piece of pipe, but you can also use a stationary jig like the one featured on page 18 (bottom right).

CENTER RIGHT
Use a hacksaw to cut through the metal spiral you have created.

BELOW LEFT
Cut one end of 8 mm/ .314 in rod to create an angled spike. Secure the metal in a vice so the flat end is almost flush with the top of the vice. Bend one of the rings so that the two open ends line up and then push the ends together. Weld the ring to the top of the rod at this point.

BELOW RIGHT
Position the second ring on the other side of the rod and weld this the same way as you did in the previous step.

ABOVE LEFT
Position the two right-angled pieces of mild steel so the shorter 70 mm/ 2.755 in side lines up with the edge of the ring, and the 80 mm/ 3.149 in side connects to the center rod. Weld the angled pieces to the rod on both sides.

ABOVE RIGHT
Carefully weld the rings to the angled pieces of metal.

ABOVE CENTER LEFT
Use a secure jig to twist a curve at each end of the 400 mm x 6 mm/ 1 ft 3.748 in length. Make sure the two ends are curved in opposite directions.

ABOVE CENTER RIGHT
The size of your curved bends will be governed by the dimensions of the jig. An offcut of pipe with an outside diameter of about 37 mm/ 1.456 in will produce a 40 mm/ 1.574 in curve.

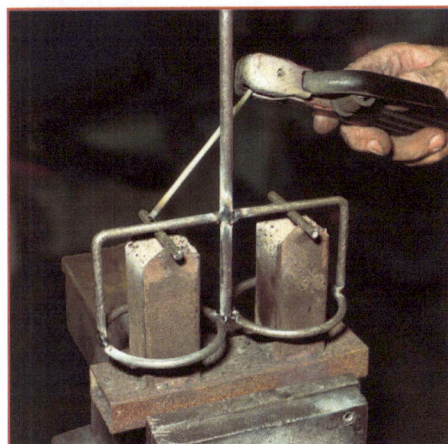

BELOW CENTER LEFT
Use a thin round file to make slight hollows in the center of one side of each of the two 80 mm/ 3.149 in lengths. Position the half-completed work securely on the workbench (this custom-made jig, also used to bend angles, is ideal) and weld the two short pieces to the framework as shown, with the filed sections joining the angled metal.

BELOW CENTER RIGHT
Weld these pieces together.

BELOW LEFT
Use a chipping hammer and then a half-round file to remove all the residual slag.

BELOW RIGHT
Finally, weld the length with curved ends on top of the stand. Chip off any slag and file clean before painting with aluminum paint or sending off for professional galvanizing (see page 33).

Finally, attach the plastic ferrules and pour yourself a drink to celebrate.

MATERIALS
– hanger –

Mild steel round bar:
  1050 mm/ 3 ft 5.338 in [6 mm/ .236 in]
Mild steel flat bar:
  130 mm x 40 mm/ 5.118 in x 1.574 in
  [2 mm/ .078 in]
Plastic ferrules:
  2 [6 mm/ .236 in]

HANDY HANGER

A useful item made for hanging on any standard door, this handy hanger can be used while ironing or as a dumb valet by you or your guests.

It is also an easy project which will improve your bending and cutting skills.

A small MMA welding machine was used for the project and the hanger was electroplated. You could also paint it or just use a black etch primer to finish it.

Basic welding tools required for this project include a bench-mounted vice and clamps to hold the metal in place; a small round file to mark the bar; a hacksaw for cutting; a bench grinder (or an angle grinder with a grinding disc) to neaten the sharp edges; a tape and soapstone chalk for measuring and marking; a ballpeen hammer to bend and to clean; and a wire brush and cold chisel, also for cleaning.

The flat metal needs to be bent so that it will slot over the door. You can make a jig from angle iron to do this yourself, or ask an engineering works to do the bending for you.

Note that it would be a good idea to measure the thickness of your doors first before bending so that they fit correctly.

LEFT
Put the round bar in the vice and use the round file to make a groove in the metal, 50 mm/ 1.968 in from one end.

RIGHT
Cut 100 mm/ 3.937 in off this same end so that the groove is now in the middle of the short bar. Later, you will weld this to the hanger to brace it against the door when in use. The groove will enable you to hold the two pieces of metal in place while you work (see facing page).

CENTER LEFT
Grind the ends of both bars on the bench grinder, to neaten the hard, sharp edges.

CENTER RIGHT
Mark the metal using soapstone chalk 150 mm/ 5.905 in from one end, to show where the bend shuld be.

BELOW LEFT
Bend the bar at the 150 mm/ 5.905 in mark, hammering it against the vice until you have formed a 90 degree angle.

BELOW RIGHT
Measure 350 mm/ 1 ft 1.779 in from the 90 degree angle and mark it with the chalk. Then bend the metal at the mark to form a triangular shape.

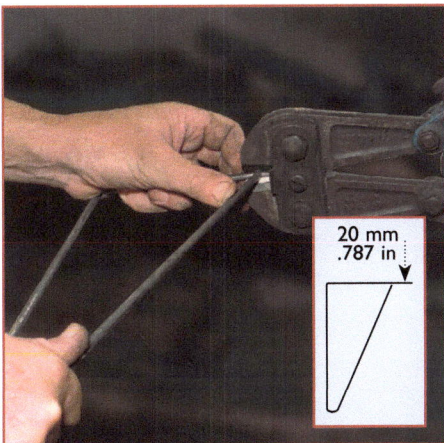

20 mm
.787 in

LEFT
Lay the triangle flat and make sure it is properly aligned. Use a bolt cutter to trim the end so that 20 mm/ .787 in extends beyond the triangle (see illustration, inset).

ABOVE RIGHT
Position the triangle in the vice and weld the opening together so that 20 mm/ .787 in of the bar extends beyond the triangle. This is what you will weld onto the flat metal which hooks onto the door.

ABOVE CENTER LEFT
Be sure to wear goggles or a mask to protect your eyes from sparks while welding.

ABOVE CENTER RIGHT
Now you can weld the short bracing crosspiece. Put this short piece of metal in the vice, with the little groove uppermost. Position the triangle at right angles to the crosspiece so that the point which forms the 90 degree angle sits in the groove.

BELOW CENTER LEFT
It is vital that the flat metal is positioned accurately at the other end. All elements must be square and the 20 mm/ .787 in extension of the bar must sit in the center of the flat metal. Spot weld the two sections before you start welding the pieces together.

BELOW CENTER RIGHT
Move the hanger to the vice and complete the weld.

BELOW LEFT
When the metal has cooled, use the cold chisel and ballpeen hammer to remove all the slag and spatter.

BELOW RIGHT
Items that are to be electro-plated must be thoroughly cleaned prior to finishing. Use a wire brush to get rid of any remaining residue. This process should also be undertaken by a professtional company. Alternatively you may just want to give the hanger a coat of self-priming etch coat.

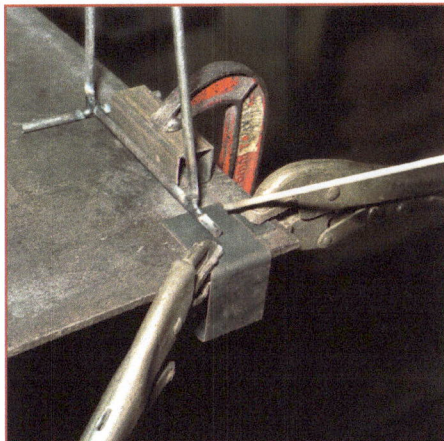

CANDLE STAND

An elegant floor standing design made to hold three rounded, chunky candles, this candle stand requires more imagination and creativity than technical skill to make. The most important part of the project is the jig that is used to bend generous curves in the metal bar. Fortunately, it is so simple to make the jig, the project may be tackled by any enthusiastic beginner with basic welding skills.

To make the jig, all you need is a piece of flat metal (30 mm x 5 mm/ 1.181 in x .196 in is ideal) which you then bend to create a circle with a 350 mm/ 1 ft 1.779 in diameter. Then you tack weld the metal to the workbench 12 mm/ .472 in from an offcut of tubing which must also be welded to the metal surface. The gap between these two pieces of metal must be accurate as this is where you will position the bar to curve it. Once you have achieved the required curve, you can use the vice (or a smaller jig)

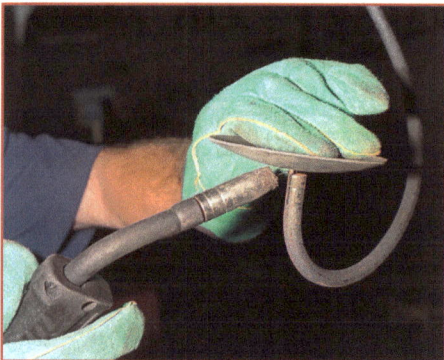

to bend the ends upwards to support the domes which hold the candles.

In addition to the vice and jig, you will need a suitable tool to cut the metal, and an MMA or MIG welding machine. A chipping hammer, angle grinder and/or files will be required to remove slag if an MMA machine is used for welding.

Any of the finishing methods may be used for this project, including special effects like verdigris (see page 34), which would be particularly effective. The candle stand shown here was powder coated.

ABOVE RIGHT
You need to bend a 30 mm x 5 mm/ 1.181 in x .196 in flat piece of metal to form a circle with a diameter of 350 mm/ 1 ft 1.779 in. To make a similar jig, spot weld a 40–50 mm/ 1.574–1.968 in-long offcut of metal tubing to the outer edge of the bench, and then tack weld the metal ring to the surface, leaving a gap of 12 mm/ .472 in between the ring and the tubing. The bar slots between the two pieces of metal and is held in place here as you bend it.

ABOVE LEFT
Bend it most of the way around the jig, to create the desired curve at one end.

CENTER RIGHT
Put the curved end of the bar into the jig and bend it upwards so that it is parallel to the straight end.

BELOW LEFT
Weld one of the domes to this end of the bar. Once the three bars have been bent and the domes welded to them, secure all three lengths in the vice, about 650 mm/ 2 ft 1.590 in from the bottom end. Twist the shortest piece of bar around all three straight ends, 500 mm/ 1 ft 7.685 in from the base to hold them together. Make about six turns and then cut off the excess. If necessary, weld to make sure it does not shift. See picture inset, above.

BELOW RIGHT
It is important that the candle end of each bar is parallel to the straight end otherwise the candle will tilt.

CANDLESTICK IDEAS

Candlesticks may be as simple or elaborate as you wish. If you favour an intricate design, consider bending scrolls and including ready-made onions and baskets in the design. A barley twist stem will add the final touch.

Some metal suppliers sell lengths of mild steel bar that have already been twisted, but once you realise how simple it is to do it yourself, you will want to give it a try. You may even decide to incorporate barley twist bars in your next gate, fence or burglar bar project.

Flat bar can be twisted very easily by clamping it into a vice on the workbench and turning it with an even movement, using a large, heavy spanner.

To twist square bar, you will have to make a jig to fit the metal you are turning. What you need to make is a long piece of metal with a square hole in it, to fit the size bar you want to twist. Then if you hold the bar steady in a vice, you can turn the jig in a circular motion to twist it.

You can make the jig with two lengths of tubing about 400 mm/ 1 ft 3.748 in long and two shorter lengths of flat metal. Position the square bar to be twisted between the ends of the tubing (this will determine the size of the hole) and clamp the flat bar on either side. Carefully remove the square bar and weld the flat bar to the tubing to complete the jig.

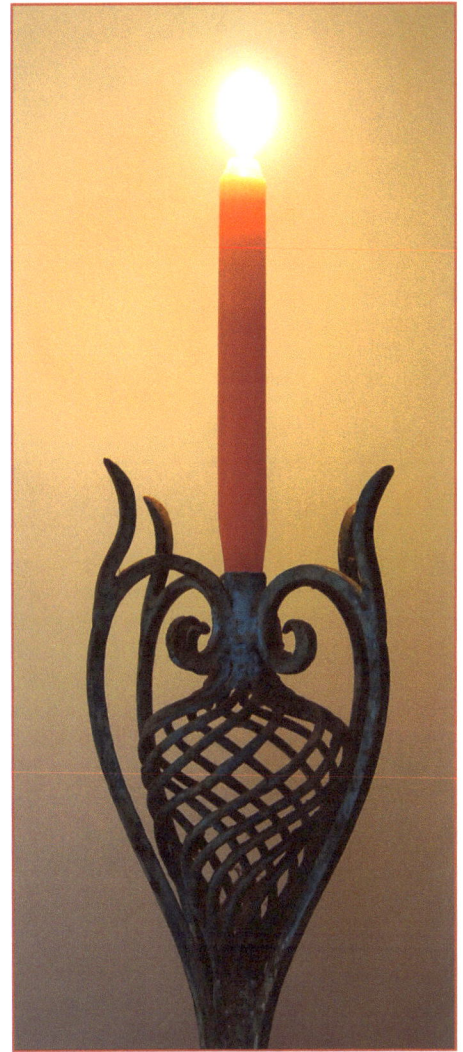

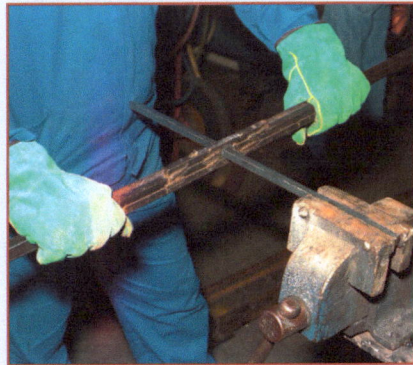

TO MAKE BARLEY TWIST BARS FROM FLAT METAL:

CENTER LEFT
Place the square bar in the bench vice with the section to be twisted protruding from the vice.

CENTER RIGHT
Slide the jig over the bar and turn it from left to right or right to left, depending whether you are left or right-handed.

BELOW LEFT
The metal will twist from the point at which it sticks out of the vice.

BELOW RIGHT
Use a large sized spanner to twist flat metal bar.

CORNER COAT RACK

A clever wall-mounted unit designed to accommodate coats, caps and other paraphernalia, is ideal for a small entrance hall or even for the corner of a covered porch.

This is a simple project which involves bending flat metal cold, and basic welding. You can bend the longer pieces of metal in a vice to create a 90 degree bend which will fit into the corner of the wall. To create the curve required for the front of the unit, bend the 720 mm/ 2 ft 4.346 in-long flat bar over a suitably curved surface (a barrel for instance).

It is best to make a jig to ensure that all the hooks are bent exactly the same way. The one used here is ingenious (see illustration below). To make your own, you will need two pieces of 25 mm/ .984 in square tubing at least 400 mm/ 1 ft 3.748 in long to form the base of the jig and the handle. Weld a shorter piece of tubing to the base, at right angles to it, and in the same plane. This supports the metal to be bent, while a stopper (a piece of tubing or flat bar smaller than the base), welded to its upper surface, holds the metal you are bending in place while you work.

Now you need to create a surface on which you can bend the metal. All you need is a piece of flat bar bent to make a circle with a 50 mm/ 1.968 in diameter (see also page 44). Weld this to the base and weld a nut onto the tubing through the center. A bolt welded to the handle screws into the nut. Mount a 30 mm/ 1.181 in (outside diameter) bearing on another bolt, on the underside of the handle, about 55 mm/ 2.165 in (center-to-center) from the pivot bolt. Make sure that the bearing and the ring are in the same horizontal plane.

To work the jig, swing the handle as far left as it will go before placing the flat bar in place on its thin edge, against the stopper. Lightly swing the arm to the right so it connects with the flat bar. Slide the flat bar forward, or backwards, to adjust the length of the bend. Swing the arm to the right, just far enough to bend the hook. Then swing the arm back to the left and remove the hook.

You will also need tools to cut the metal. A plasma cutter is ideal as it will give you a good, clean edge on the expanded metal. A hack saw or 'cut-off' machine may be used to cut the flat bar. You will need an angle grinder or a bench grinder to smooth and round off the ends of the hooks, and clamps to hold the metal while you bend and weld it. A drill or drill press is required to make holes in the thicker (30 mm/ 1.181 in) flat bar to enable you to screw the unit to the wall.

A small MMA welding machine is all you need to weld the coat rack. A chipping hammer, angle grinder and/or files will be required to remove any slag and spatter.

This rack has been spray painted using ordinary aerosol cans of primer and paint.

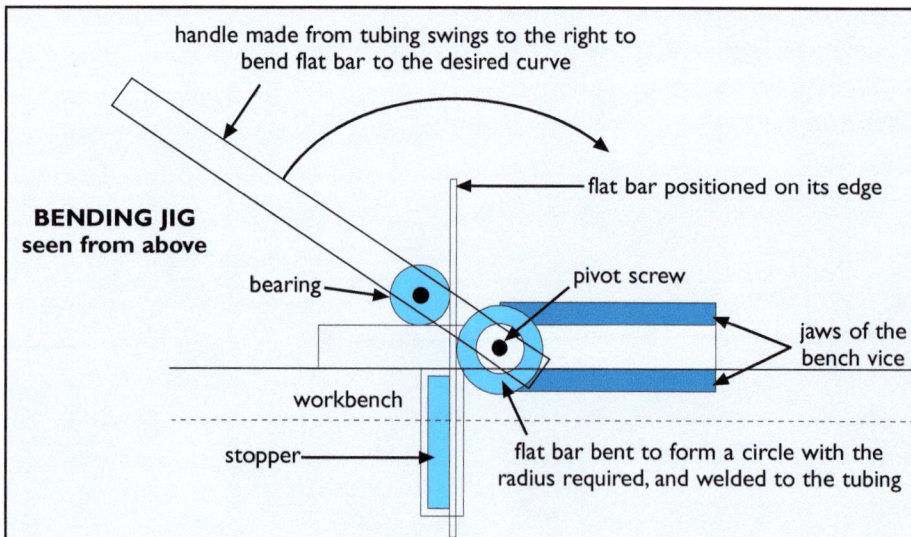

handle made from tubing swings to the right to
bend flat bar to the desired curve

BENDING JIG
seen from above

flat bar positioned on its edge

bearing

pivot screw

jaws of the
bench vice

workbench

stopper

flat bar bent to form a circle with the
radius required, and welded to the tubing

RIGHT
Plan for an ingenious jig that will enable you to bend metal (including the hooks) to create the exact curve you want.

ABOVE LEFT
Cut all the metal to size and then bend the bar which forms the framework of the coat rack as well as the hooks. Grind the ends of the hooks so they are smooth and rounded.

ABOVE RIGHT
A 'cut-off' machine is ideal for cutting the flat metal bar.

ABOVE CENTER LEFT
The two 900 mm/ 2 ft 11.433 in lengths of flat bar are bent at a 90 degree angle, in the center. Position each one in the vice at the halfway mark and then bend it firmly towards you. This is where the rack fits into the corner of the wall.

ABOVE CENTER RIGHT
Use the bending jig to form the four hooks.

BELOW CENTER LEFT
Before you weld the hooks to the two bent lengths, drill a hole about 50 mm/ 1.968 in from each end of the thicker bar. Drill another couple of holes towards the corner on each side so you can bolt the rack to the wall later. Position the bars 100 mm/ 3.937 in apart and clamp the first hook to one end. Make sure the ends are aligned and that the two bars remain parallel. Weld the hook and bar together.

BELOW CENTER RIGHT
Position the second hook about 200 mm/ 7.874 in from the first one; clamp it to the bar and weld. Weld the other two hooks to the other side of the two bars, the same distance apart.

BELOW LEFT
Clamp the curved front rail to the side pieces and weld them together.

BELOW RIGHT
Clamp and weld the expanded metal to the top of the coat rack.

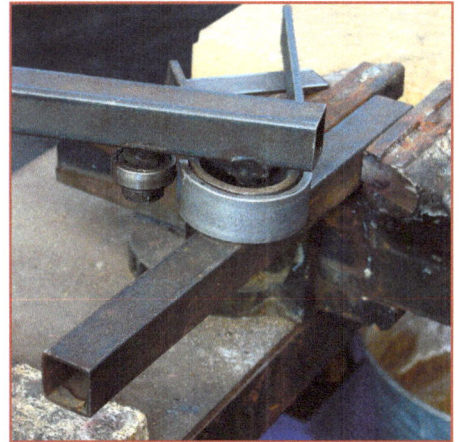

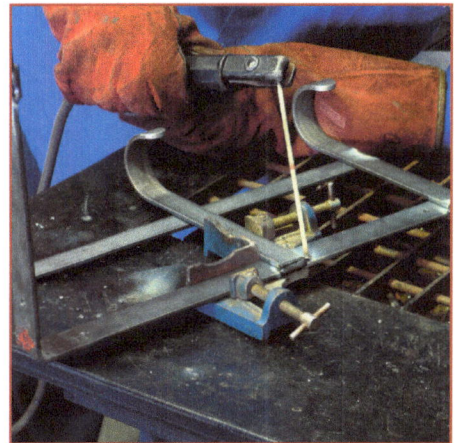

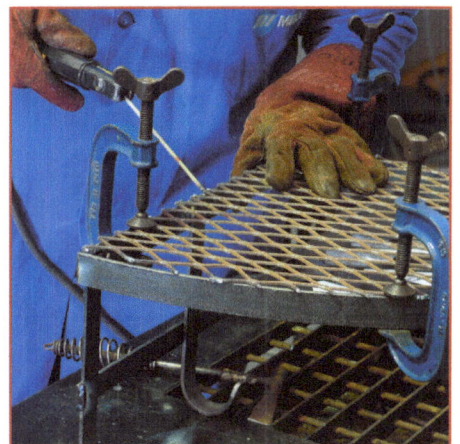

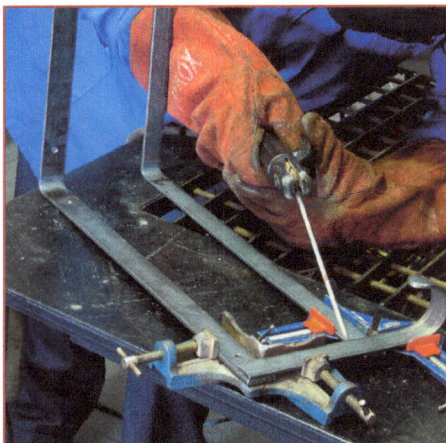

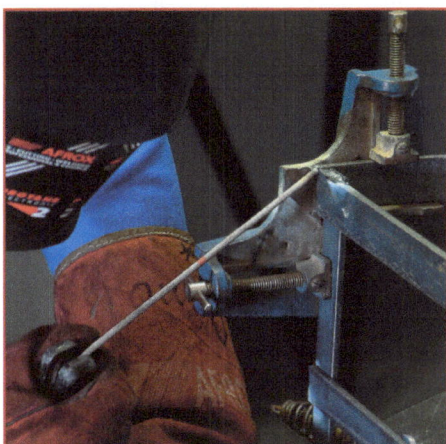

GLASS-TOPPED TABLE

A small decorative table, suitable for use anywhere in the house or on the patio, is made from square tubing and flat bar and topped with smoked glass. Instead of glass, you could screw chipboard to the upper surface of the frame and tile the top, perhaps with handpainted ceramic tiles.

This is a project which can easily be completed in a single weekend. Making the table involves cutting the tubing correctly, bending the flat metal to create a decorative pattern which will also brace the frame, and welding the pieces together correctly.

You will need a small MMA welding machine, although a MIG welder, or even gas welding equipment could be used instead. You can use a hacksaw to cut the flat metal and most of the tubing. Where 45 degree angles are required, you will produce a more accurate cut if you use a bench-mounted, hand-operated mitre saw. Since it is essential that the cuts and joins are done correctly, make sure you have an engineer's square on hand to check these. Clamps are essential tools for this project, and you will need a chipping hammer to remove any slag

or spatter, and files to clean and dress the welds and ensure there are no sharp edges. You can use any finish for the table, depending on whether you plan to use it inside or in the garden. This one was given an initial undercoat of grey primer sprayed from an aerosol can. The final sprayed coat was matt black.

Start by cleaning the metal to remove any oil and then cut all the lengths to size, making sure the legs and lower rails are cut off square, and the ends of the top rails are cut to a 45 degree angle. Once the table is assembled, the internal measurement from corner-to-corner should be 400 mm/ 1 ft 3.748 in.

The ends of the four gussets which support the upper frame (top rails) of the table, must also be cut at a 45 degree angle. Note that the tubing used for the lower rail is slightly shorter than the top rails as it slots against the legs and is welded to them. The flat metal used to brace the framework must be bent to form curved (or bow)

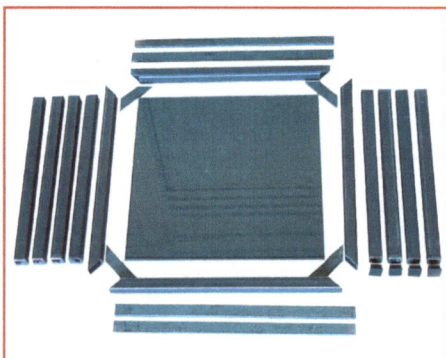

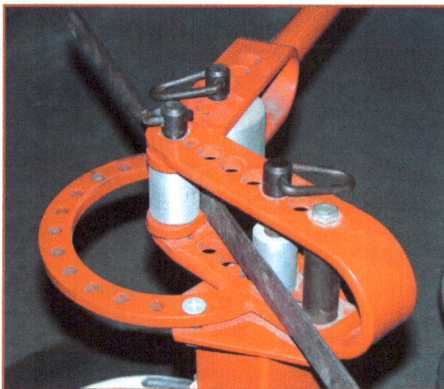

ABOVE
A bending machine is handy when bending a number of pieces that have to have an identical shape.

BELOW LEFT
Cut all the metal to size before you start. It is essential that the glass is the correct size for the design. If you are in any doubt, complete the table and then measure for the glass afterwards; this will allow for any minor inaccuracies.

BELOW RIGHT
The completed table, spray painted and with the smoked glass in place.

shapes, 100 mm/ 3.937 in high and measuring 400 mm/ 1 ft 3.748 in from end-to-end.

Use right-angled clamps to assemble the upper frame. Check that all four corners are square and that the internal measurements are 400 mm/ 1 ft 3.748 in from corner to corner. Tack weld the joints before clamping the legs to the framework, then tack welding these. The lower rails should be welded between the legs, 100 mm/ 3.937 in below the upper frame; this is where the bow-shaped bracing must be welded. Finally, the gussets are welded across the corners, under the upper section of the framework.

Once the table is complete and has been spray painted, press end plugs into the bottom of each of the legs. Place the table upright, and carefully drop the smoked glass top into place.

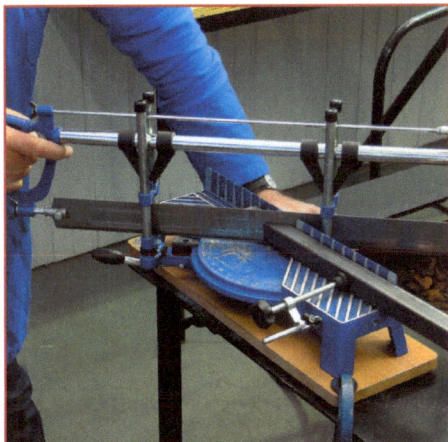

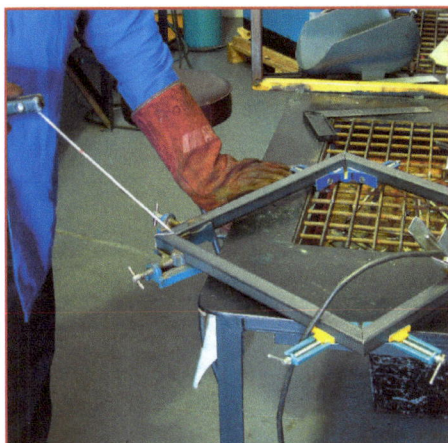

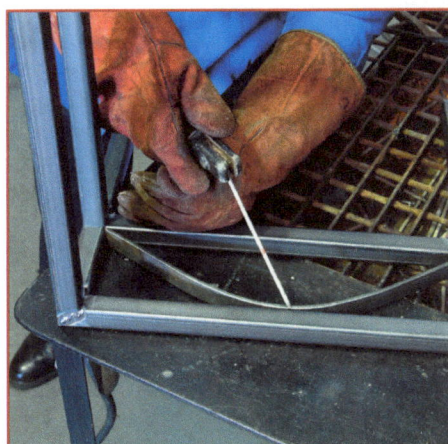

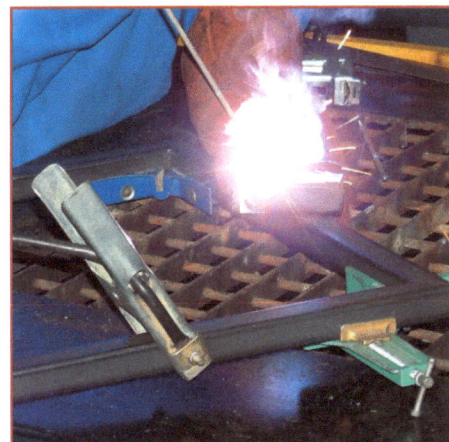

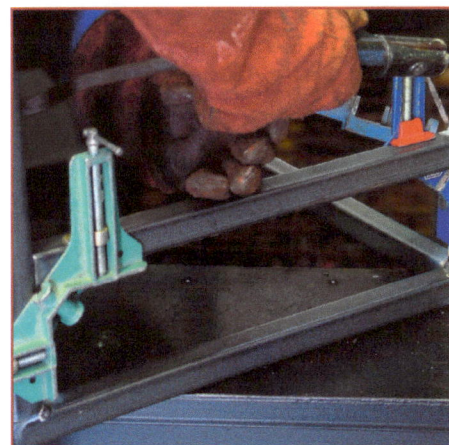

ABOVE LEFT
Cut the ends of the top rails at 45 degrees using a bench-mounted mitre saw.

ABOVE RIGHT
Clamp two of the top rails together to form a mitred joint and weld the sections together.

ABOVE CENTER LEFT
Clamp and weld the other three corners.

ABOVE CENTER RIGHT
When welding, do not forget to wear gloves to protect your hands and a welding helmet with a correctly shaded lens.

BELOW CENTER LEFT
Clamp the legs in position, ready for welding.

BELOW CENTER RIGHT
Once you tack welded the legs to the upper frame, clamp and tack weld the lower rails in place.

BELOW LEFT
Weld the bow-shaped flat metal between the two rails, with the curved section uppermost. Then weld the gussets across the corners on the underside of the upper rails.

BELOW RIGHT
Once the entire framework has been tack welded you can complete the welding operation. When the metal has cooled down, clean all the welds and spray-paint the table using primer and top coat, rubbing the surface gently with fine water paper between coats.

MATERIALS
– gate –

Mild steel pipe:
  1 x 900 mm/ 2 ft 11.433 in
  [50 mm/ 1.968 in]
  1 x 1,36 m/ 4 ft 5.543 in [50 mm/ 1.968 in]
Mild steel flat metal:
  1 x 740 mm/ 2 ft 5.133 in;
  1 x 700 mm/ 2 ft 3.559 in;
  [40 mm x 5 mm/ 1.574 in x .196 in]
Mild steel round bar, 8 mm/ .314 in:
  1,1 m/ 3 ft 7.307 in; 1,2 m/ 3 ft 11.244 in;
  1,3 m/ 4 ft 3.181 in; 1,4 m/ 4 ft 7.118 in;
  1,5 m/ 4 ft 11.055 in; 1,6 m/ 5 ft 2.992 in
Cast iron balls:
  3 x 30 mm/ 1.181 in, 2 x 35 mm/ 1.377 in,
  2 x 40 mm/ 1.574 in, 1 x 50 mm/ 1.968 in
Mild steel domes:
  2 x 50 mm/ 1.968 in
Gate hinges: 2
Barrel bolt: 1

GARDEN GATE

This unusual gate has architectural features which make it very different to the average garden gate. However, it is not a difficult item to make, requiring only basic bending and welding skills.

The design features a series of mild steel metal bars which have been randomly bent, curled, flattened at the bottom, and topped with different sized cast iron balls. The bars are different lengths and arranged from lowest to highest, between two lengths of pipe which, in effect, create the frame for the gate. These elements are attached to two pieces of flat metal which have been hammered to give a beaten appearance, and then bent to curve them slightly.

You can use any arc welding machine to make the gate, even though the step-by-step project shows MIG welding equipment.

You will also need a hacksaw or suitable power tool to cut the bar to size; a bench-mounted vice; and jigs for bending the bars and flat metal. An anvil is the ideal surface on which to hammer the flat metal, otherwise use any solid surface. You will need a ball peen hammer to beat the metal.

If you use an MMA machine, you will also need the usual chipping hammer, files and grinders to remove slag, and clean and dress the metal. An electric drill, suitable spanners, and a tape measure and spirit level will be needed when it comes to hanging the gate.

A hardy finish is essential for any garden gate. This one was galvanized and then epoxy coated.

ABOVE RIGHT
Hammer both sides of the flat metal with the ball peen hammer to give it texture.

CENTER LEFT
Hammer the ends of six metal bars, to flatten about 5 mm/ .196 in.

CENTER RIGHT
Use a suitable jig (or pipe) to bend the bar in circles to create two curls in each one. These should be in different places in each bar so that some curls are above the flat metal crosspieces and some below. Instead of leaving the rest of the bar completely straight, bend them randomly for effect. You do not need a jig to do this, just bend the metal over your knee.

BELOW LEFT
You will need a jig to bend the flat metal. Make this with two 50–60 mm/ 1.968 in–2.362 in offcuts of angle iron set 150 mm/ 5.905 in apart.

BELOW RIGHT
Weld balls to the tops of the vertical bars and a dome and one ball to the top of each outside pipe. Finally weld the bars and the pipe to the bars. Once the metal has been galvanized and/or epoxy coated or painted, you can hang the gate.

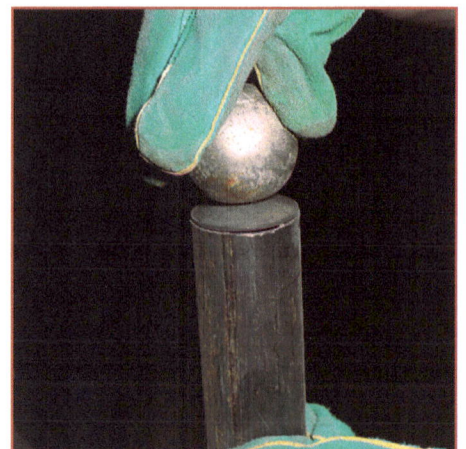

GATE OR BALUSTRADE IDEA

To make gates or fences try to alternate straight lengths and curved pieces.

To ensure each bar is bent exactly the same way, you will need a jig. Make this with short pieces of 30 mm x 5 mm/ 1.181 in x .196 in flat metal, bent to form curves and welded onto another wide, long piece of metal. All vertical bars are 12 mm/ .472 in; the pipe dividing each panel is 38 mm/ 1.496 in; the flat metal at the top is 38 mm x 19 mm/ 1.496 in x .748 in, and the metal at the base is 32 mm x 19 mm/ 1.259 in x 1.496 in.

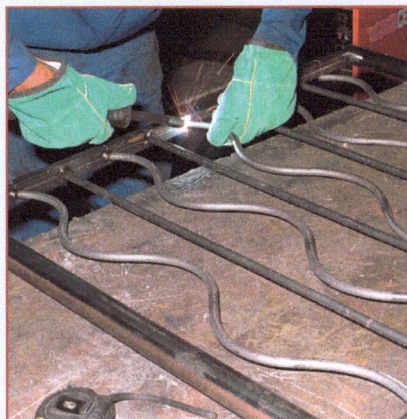

CENTER LEFT
The secret of this design lies in the jig. This one is made with a series of curved pieces of flat metal. Since each of these must be exactly the same, you will, of course, need something which has the required curve to bend these on before they are welded to the base metal. Use a pipe or any suitably sized chunk of scrap metal. You will also need to weld an offcut of some sort at the end, to keep the end in place.

CENTER RIGHT
Bend the bar along and around the jig to complete the series of curves.

BELOW RIGHT
Weld straight and curved round bar between the flat metal which forms the top and bottom of the gate or balustrade. If you are making a balustrade, it is a good idea to cover the top section of metal with wood to finish it off neatly.

MATERIALS
– burglar bars –

Mild steel round bar:
  1 x 340 mm/ 1 ft 1.385 in,
  1 x 360 mm/ 1 ft 2.173 in,
  2 x 680 mm/ 2 ft 2.771 in,
  2 x 780 mm/ 2 ft 6.708 in
  2 x 900 mm/ 2 ft 11.433 in [16 mm/ .629 in]
Cast iron spears:
  5 x 106 mm/ 4.173 in [44 mm/ 1.732 in]
Cast iron balls:
  5 x 40 mm/ 1.574 in
Mild steel onion:
  1 x 12 mm/ .472 in [6 mm/ .236 in]
Mild steel rings:
  7 x 16 mm/ .629 in inside diameter
  [6 mm/ .236 in]
Coach bolts with snap off head and plugs:
  4 x 75 mm/ 2.952 in [10 mm/ .393 in]

BURGLAR BARS

These attractive burglar bars may be made to any dimension, to fit any window size. You can even use the basic spearhead design for gates and fences.

Materials specified above will enable you to produce burglar bars that will fit a window approximately 600 mm/ 1 ft 11.622 in wide and 650 mm/ 2 ft 1.590 in deep, and may also be used across a narrow 500 mm/1 ft 7.685 in-wide, 900 mm/ 2 ft 11.433 in long window as shown in the picture on the right.

This project shows the bars being welded together with a MIG welding machine; you can also use an MMA machine.

You will also need a hacksaw, angle grinder, band saw or 'cut-off' machine to cut the bar to size; a vice for bending the metal and holding it steady on the workbench; and a bench-mounted drill or drill press (and a 12 mm/ .472 in steel drill bit) to make holes in the domes to accommodate the coach bolts. An offcut piece of square tubing will enable you to bend the end of the bar accurately, without curving the rest of it. The tubing should have an inside diameter large enough to slot over the 16 mm/ .629 in bar.

If you use a MMA machine, you will also need files to finish off the job.

Since burglar bars are exposed to all weather conditions, choose a finish which will withstand the elements. These bars were galvanized to prevent any possibility of rust, and then powder coated.

ABOVE RIGHT
Several bought items are used to make the burglar bars including the onion, cast iron balls and spears, and the domes which enable you easily mount the bars on the wall. The rings are made from 6 mm/ .236 in mild steel bar.

CENTER LEFT
To make the rings, bend the 6 mm/ .236 in bar around the 16 mm/ .629 in bar (or use a jig with an outside diameter of 16 mm/ .629 in). Make sure it is a good, tight fit and there are no gaps.

CENTER RIGHT
Remove the 6 mm/ .236 in metal spiral from the thicker bar and use a 'cut-off' machine to cut through the metal to create rings.

BELOW LEFT
Cut the 16 mm/ .629 in bar to size. A 'cut-off' machine will enable you to do this quickly and effortlessly.

BELOW RIGHT
Bend both ends of the two 900 mm/ 2 ft 11.433 in-long bars 150 mm/ 5.905 in from each end, to form a 45 degree angle. Position the metal bar in the vice and slot the tubing over the bar prior to bending.

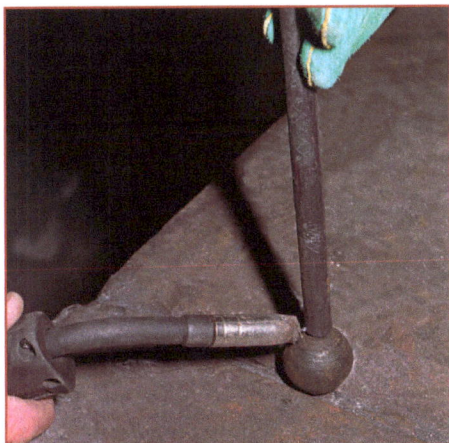

ABOVE LEFT
The balls must be welded to one end of each bar. As the trigger of the MIG torch is pulled, the wire starts to feed.

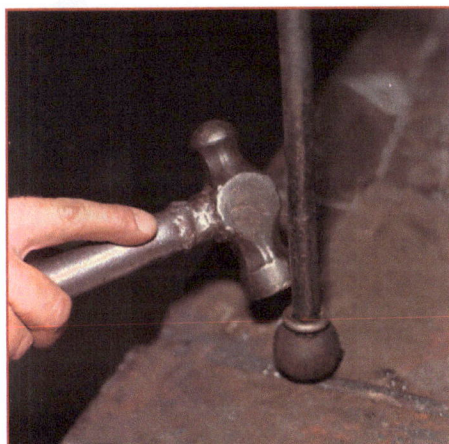

ABOVE RIGHT
As the wire strikes the joint, the arc, which is protected from the atmosphere by the shielding gas, is established, and you can weld the two elements together.

ABOVE CENTER LEFT
Push a ring over the other end of the bar and hammer it gently until it sits just above the ball. Be careful not to bend the ring.

ABOVE CENTER RIGHT
Weld the spears to the ends of the 680 mm/ 2 ft 2.771 in-, 780 mm/ 2 ft 6.708 in- and 340 mm/ 1 ft 1.385 in-long bars. Note that most off-the-shelf spears are manufactured for use with 12 mm/ .472 in bar. This means the 16 mm/ .629 in bar will not slot into the hollow base; but this does not matter as the weld will hold the pieces together. You will also have to weld the onion between the open ends of the 340 mm/ 1 ft 1.385 in- and 360 mm/ 1 ft 2.173 in-long bars, with a ring on each side of the onion.

BELOW CENTER LEFT
Weld domes to each end of the bars you previously bent. The join should not be in the center as this is where you will need to drill to accommodate the bolts.

BELOW CENTER RIGHT
Use a 12 mm/ .472 in twist steel drill bit to make holes in the center of the domes.

BELOW LEFT
Weld the bars topped with spears to the two crosspieces.

BELOW RIGHT
Note that the onion is welded between the shorter bars, with a ring on each side of the onion.

BURGLAR BAR IDEA

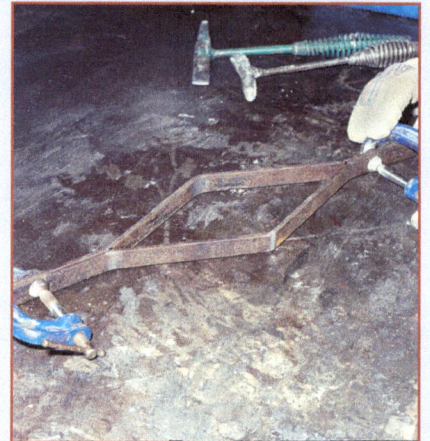

These ingenious burglar bars were made with 20 mm x 5 mm/ .787 in x .196 in flat bar, bent to create a diamond shape and then welded together to form an intriguing pattern.

If you cut a small notch halfway through the metal it will be easier to bend. Each side of the diamond should be 150 mm/ 5.905 in long.

ABOVE RIGHT
Cut the metal to size and mark the position of the bends. To create the diamond pattern shown here, they should be 150 mm/ 5.905 in apart.

ABOVE CENTER RIGHT
Once you have bent the bar (see page 18), clamp two pieces together to form a diamond shape.

CENTER LEFT
If you are working on a metal workbench, clamp the return lead to the work bench to earth it.

CENTER RIGHT
Weld the sections together.

BELOW LEFT
Once the metal cools down, use a chipping hammer to remove all the residual slag from the surface of the joins.

BELOW RIGHT
Use an angle grinder to smooth the surface of the joins. Once you have made all the diamond shapes, weld these together with additional flat metal to make the burglar bars.

HEXAGONAL FIREPLACE

This attractive, freestanding hexagonal fireplace, made mainly from 3 mm/ .118 in mild steel sheet metal, is a time consuming project, but the processes involved are reasonably straightforward.

All the metal should be cut to size, before you start welding. Use the illustrations on page 56 to make cardboard templates, and then either cut the metal yourself using a plasma cutter, or take your templates to an engineering works and ask them to do it for you. The round and square bar can be cut with a 'cut-off' machine, or even with an ordinary hacksaw.

Bending of the flat metal and round bar can be done using a bench vice. Welding can be done with any suitable MMA machine, or with a MIG welding machine. Both were used for this project which was undertaken at a technical training college.

You will also need a chipping hammer and an angle grinder or grinding machine to remove spatter and slag from the welded joints.

There are some similarities between this project and the built-in barbecue featured on pages 58–61; follow the barbecue instructions to complete the cowl. A flat piece of metal is welded to the top end of the flue (see page 57) and a short, 100 mm/3.937 in-long piece of 10 mm/ .393 in (internal diameter) pipe is welded to the center of this. The pin on the cowl then slots into the protruding pipe (see page 61).

Finish the fireplace by painting with an etch primer or a suitable heat resistant paint.

MATERIALS
– fireplace –
(Imperial decimal sizes)

Mild steel sheet:
  .118 in, cut according to the illustrations for the fireplace;
  2 x 3 ft 11.244 in x 3.937 in for the flue;
  1 x 1 ft 7.685 in x 1 ft 7.685 in for the ashtray;
  1 x 1 ft 7.685 in x 1 ft 7.685 in for the cowl
Mild steel flat bar:
  2 x 1 ft 6.503 in; 1 x 1 ft 2.960 in;
  2 x 11.220 in; 1 x 8.346 in
  [.984 in x .196 in] for the trim;
  2 x 1 ft 6.897 in; 1 x 1 ft 3.354 in;
  2 x 11.614 in; 1 x 8.740 in [.984 in x .196 in];
  2 x .787 in [.393 in x .196 in] for the screen;
  1 x 7.874 in [.984 in x .196 in] for the flue;
  1 x 1 ft 3.748 in; 7 x 1 ft 5.716 in;
  2 x 1 ft 2.960 in; 1 x 1 ft 1.385 in;
  1 x 10.236 in [2.047 in x .196 in] for the grate.
Mild steel round bar:
  1 x 9.055 in [.196 in] for the screen handle
Mild steel square bar
  1 x 1 ft 5.716 in [.393 in x .393 in] for the grate
Mild steel flat bar with swivel hinge:
  1 x 8.661 in [.984 in x .196 in]
Mild steel diamond mesh:
  2 ft 11.433 in x 1 ft 5.716
  [.984 in x .472 in]

See table for metric sizes on page 63

ABOVE LEFT
These are first pieces you will need to start welding.

CENTER LEFT
The completed fireplace with the safety screen and grate.

BELOW CENTER LEFT
It is a good idea to cut the metal to size before you start welding. You can do it yourself with a plasma cutter, which cuts cleanly and neatly, producing an edge which is easy to weld.

LEFT
The side pieces fit along the edge of the hexagonal base like a simple puzzle.

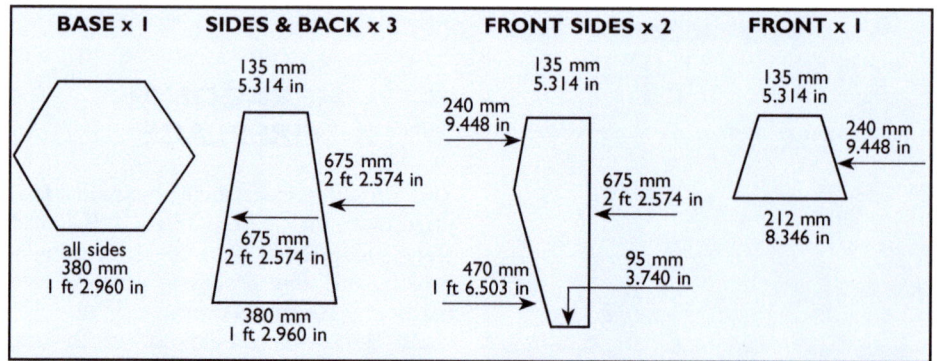

BASE x 1	SIDES & BACK x 3	FRONT SIDES x 2	FRONT x 1

BASE x 1

all sides
380 mm
1 ft 2.960 in

SIDES & BACK x 3

135 mm
5.314 in

675 mm
2 ft 2.574 in

675 mm
2 ft 2.574 in

675 mm
2 ft 2.574 in

380 mm
1 ft 2.960 in

FRONT SIDES x 2

135 mm
5.314 in

240 mm
9.448 in

675 mm
2 ft 2.574 in

470 mm
1 ft 6.503 in

95 mm
3.740 in

FRONT x 1

135 mm
5.314 in

240 mm
9.448 in

212 mm
8.346 in

ABOVE RIGHT
Assemble the hexagonal section by tack welding (or tacking) the inside edges at several points no more than 50–100 mm/ 1.968 in–3.937 in apart.

ABOVE FAR RIGHT
Tack weld the outside edges in the same way, at different points. This will hold the sections together while you continue work.

CENTER RIGHT
Once you have tack welded all the sides to the base, turn the hexagonal section upside down and weld the foot to the center of the base. Note that the foot is made from two lengths of metal, each bent twice and welded together to form a hollow hexagonal section (see illustration below).

RIGHT
The foot has been tack welded to the base. Note the points at which the 130 mm/ 5.118 in ends have been welded to form lap joints on two of the six sides.

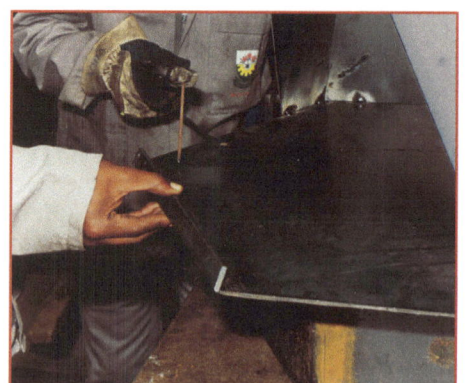

FAR RIGHT
Once you have welded the front to the hexagonal section, weld the flat bar (trim) to the edges around the opening to finish it off. The shortest 212 mm/ 8.346 in piece fits across the top of the opening, at the bottom of the front section; and the 380 mm/ 1 ft 2.960 in length fits across the base of the opening. The remaining four lengths will enable you to finish off the entire opening.

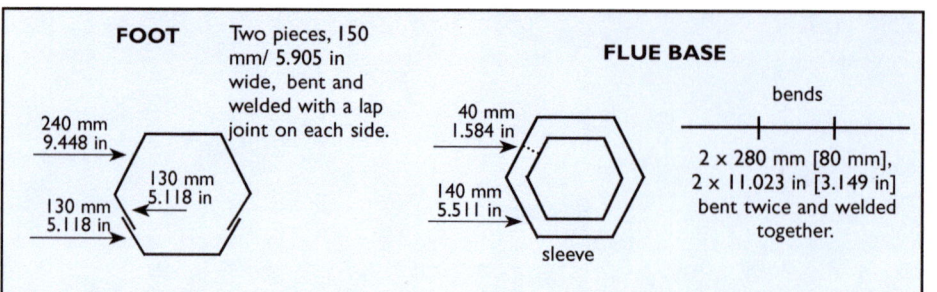

FOOT

Two pieces, 150 mm/ 5.905 in wide, bent and welded with a lap joint on each side.

240 mm
9.448 in

130 mm
5.118 in

130 mm
5.118 in

FLUE BASE

40 mm
1.584 in

140 mm
5.511 in

sleeve

bends

2 x 280 mm [80 mm],
2 x 11.023 in [3.149 in]
bent twice and welded together.

ASHTRAY

GRATE

500 mm
1 ft 7.685 in

50 x 50 mm
1.968 x 1.968 in
cut out of each
corner

bend along
dotted lines

380 mm
1 ft 2.960 in

340 mm
1 ft 1.385 in

260 mm
10.236 in

400 mm
1 ft 3.748 in

260 mm
10.236 in

7 x 430 mm
7 x 1 ft 4.949 in
bent to shape

250 mm
9.842 in

450 mm
1 ft 5.716 in

950 mm
3 ft 1.401 in

ABOVE LEFT

Complete the base for the flue by tack welding the 40 mm/ 1.574 in-wide sleeve to the top of the fireplace. Bend the two 280 mm x 80 mm/ 11.023 in x 3.149 in lengths of metal in two places, as indicated in the illustration on page 56, at 120 degrees. Weld the two hexagonal pieces together. This section can then be spot welded to the top of the fireplace.

TOP RIGHT

The safety screen is made with diamond mesh and flat bar which is slightly longer than the metal used to finish the open edges of the fireplace. Cut the mesh to size and bend at 120 degree angles so you can slot the screen neatly across the front. Bend a 90 degree angle, 50 mm/ 1.968 in from each end of the 230 mm/ 9.055 in long round bar, to form a handle; weld this to the top of the screen. Weld the two 20 mm x 10 mm/ .787 in x .393 in bits of bar to the base of the screen, 60 mm/ 2.362 in from each corner, to form hooks to keep it in place.

CENTER LEFT

The safety screen should slot neatly over the opening.

ABOVE CENTER RIGHT

Once the fireplace has been assembled and tack welded, you can complete the welding operation.

BELOW LEFT

Use an angle grinder to smooth all the rough edges.

BELOW CENTER RIGHT

Assemble and weld the flue and then chip off any slag. Weld the flat bar across the opening to support the cowl.

BELOW

Following the illustrations, left, bend and weld the flat metal to form the ashtray and the flat and square bar for the grate.

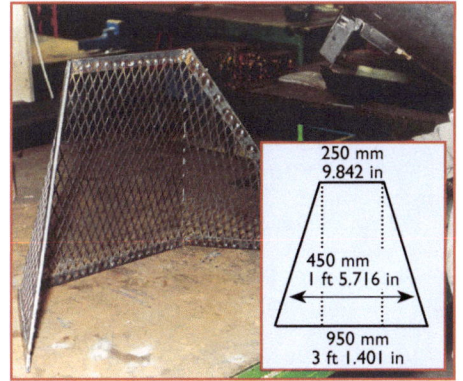

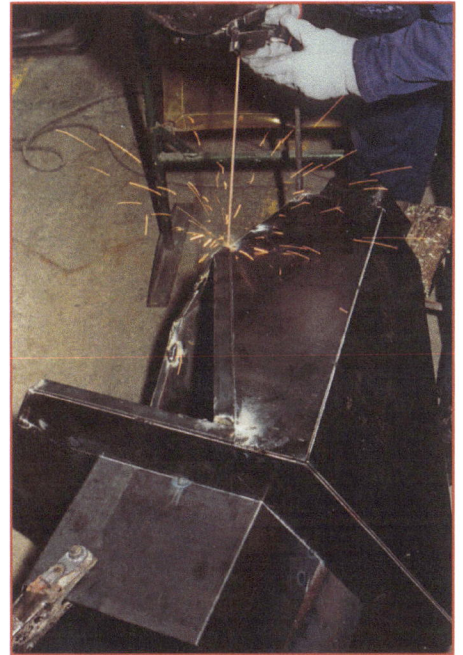

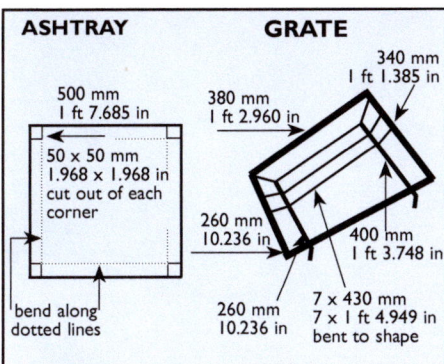

BUILT-IN BARBECUE

A fulfilling but complicated project, this built-in barbecue unit should only be tackled by welders with some experience. It is made with large sheets of metal which must be accurately bent according to plan before the various elements are welded together. Not only are edges bent, but the back and base (made from a single sheet of metal) also incorporate bends which give the unit rigidity.

LEFT
If you are cutting and bending your own metal, measure and mark all the sheets before you start.

RIGHT
A large guillotine is ideal for sheet metal, but not the kind of equipment a weekend welder will have. For a project of this scale it may be advisable to ask your metal merchant to cut the sheets when you order the metal.

The easiest way to cut and bend the sheets is with special bending and cutting machines. Weekend welders will not have this equipment, so it is a good idea to order the materials cut to size and bent according to plan. You could cut the sheet using a plasma cutter at home, and the flat and round bar can be cut with a handsaw or 'cut off' machine.

Either a MIG welding machine, or an MMA machine may be used to weld the sections of the barbecue together.

The smaller elements can be welded on a workbench, using a bench vice and clamps to position them for welding. However, the scale of the barbecue itself means you will have to do quite a lot of the work on the floor. This means that the workpiece must be earthed. It also means that you will need to get some extra hands to help you hold

the cut sheets together while you tack weld the pieces together.

The folding shelf which is held in place by thin chains in front of the cooking area, is optional. Materials are specified for this and for a second section which will close the front completely.

Once the entire unit has been tack welded, weld between the tacks to form solid joints. Allow the metal to cool and then clean all welds and smooth any rough edges. Use a chipping hammer to get rid of slag and spatter and an angle grinder to smooth rough edges. Paint the barbecue with an etch primer before installing it.

BACK AND BASE SECTION

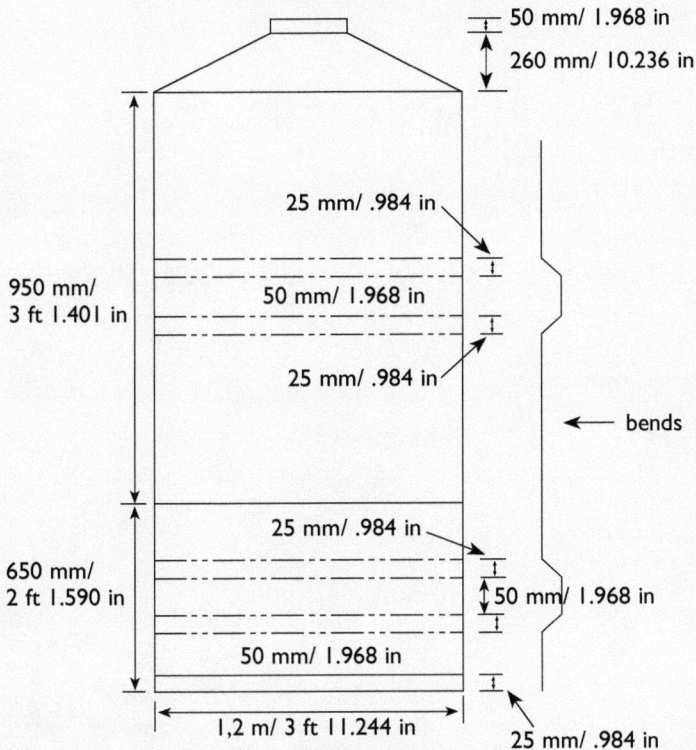

50 mm/ 1.968 in
260 mm/ 10.236 in
25 mm/ .984 in
50 mm/ 1.968 in
25 mm/ .984 in
← bends
950 mm/ 3 ft 1.401 in
25 mm/ .984 in
650 mm/ 2 ft 1.590 in
50 mm/ 1.968 in
50 mm/ 1.968 in
1,2 m/ 3 ft 11.244 in
25 mm/ .984 in

FRONT SECTION

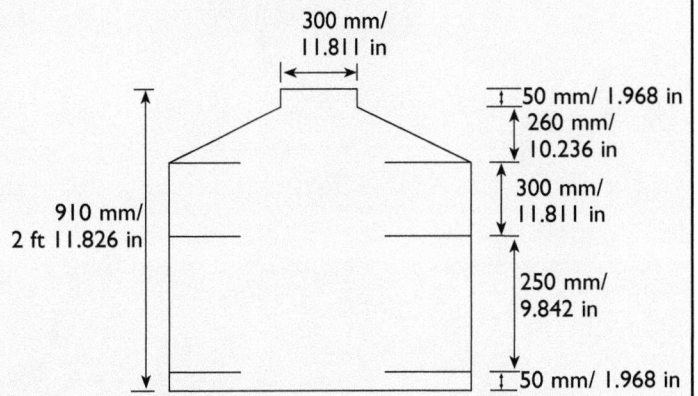

300 mm/ 11.811 in
50 mm/ 1.968 in
260 mm/ 10.236 in
300 mm/ 11.811 in
910 mm/ 2 ft 11.826 in
250 mm/ 9.842 in
50 mm/ 1.968 in

TOP OF FRONT x 2

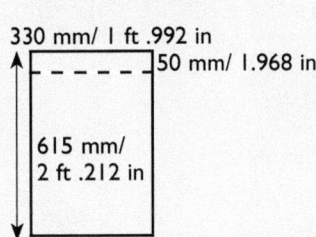

330 mm/ 1 ft .992 in
50 mm/ 1.968 in
615 mm/ 2 ft .212 in

SIDES

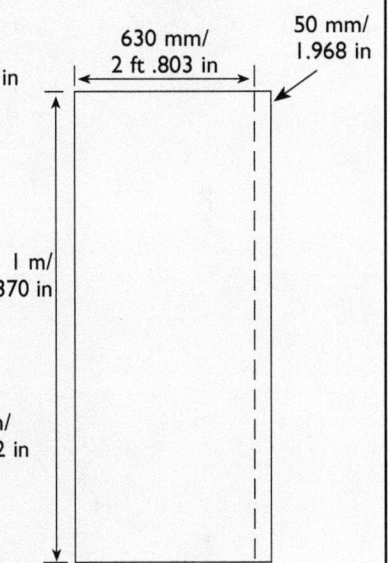

630 mm/ 2 ft .803 in
50 mm/ 1.968 in
1 m/ 3 ft 3.370 in

BOTTOM OF FRONT x 2

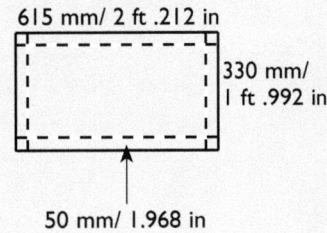

615 mm/ 2 ft .212 in
330 mm/ 1 ft .992 in
50 mm/ 1.968 in

ASH PAN

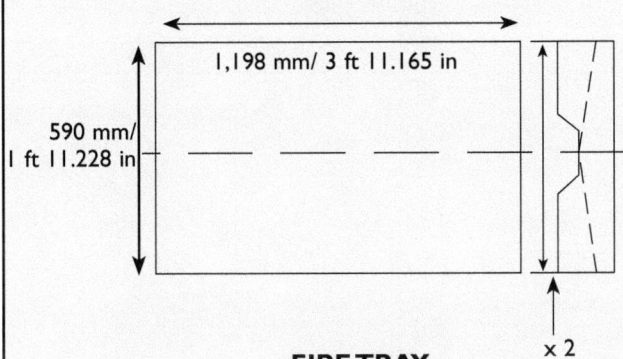

1,198 mm/ 3 ft 11.165 in
590 mm/ 1 ft 11.228 in
x 2

FIRE TRAY

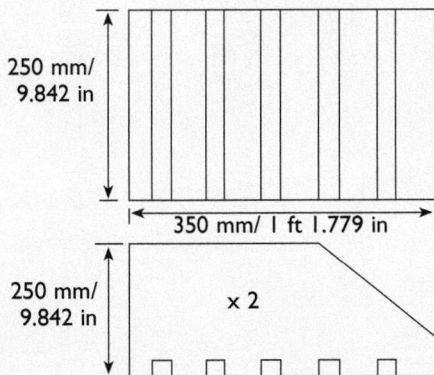

250 mm/ 9.842 in
350 mm/ 1 ft 1.779 in
250 mm/ 9.842 in
x 2

Cut a 3rd piece 275 mm x 250 mm/ 10.826 in x 9.842 in for the back of the fire tray.

BARBECUE GRID

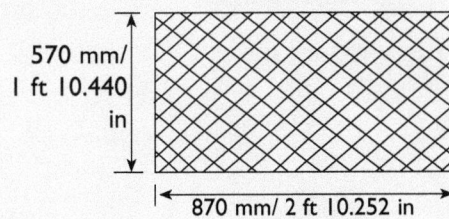

570 mm/ 1 ft 10.440 in
870 mm/ 2 ft 10.252 in

COWL

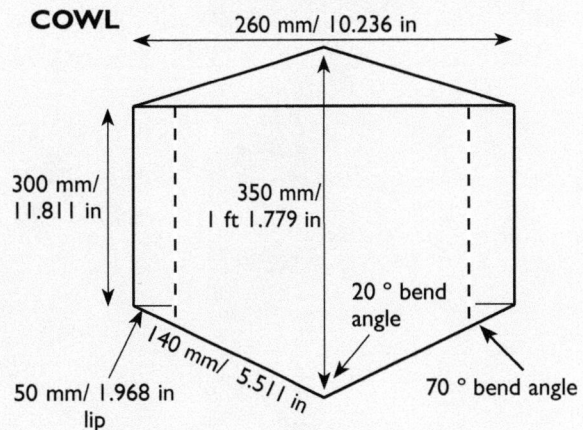

260 mm/ 10.236 in
300 mm/ 11.811 in
350 mm/ 1 ft 1.779 in
20 ° bend angle
140 mm/ 5.511 in
50 mm/ 1.968 in lip
70 ° bend angle

BEAK OF COWL

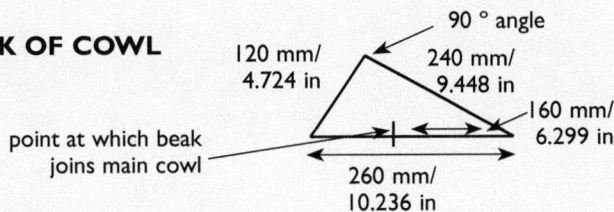

90 ° angle
120 mm/ 4.724 in
240 mm/ 9.448 in
160 mm/ 6.299 in
point at which beak joins main cowl
260 mm/ 10.236 in

ABOVE LEFT

If you are going to cut the sheets yourself, use a plasma cutter. Mark the cutting line clearly with soapstone chalk.

ABOVE RIGHT

A large bending machine will bend the metal sheet quickly and accurately. You can outsource this part of the project and ask a metal merchant or welding shop to do it for you.

CENTER LEFT

Assemble the barbecue unit systematically and tack weld the pieces together. Start with the back (which is also bent to form the base) and the two side pieces.

ABOVE CENTER RIGHT

The two pieces labelled 'top of front' slot in to complete the base of the flue.

BELOW LEFT

The base of the ash pan is bent along the center to form a 20 degree bend. Also bend 50 mm/ 1.968 in of the two long edges upwards at about 70 degrees. The two end pieces are then welded to the shorter ends.

BELOW CENTER RIGHT

Bend about 25 mm/ .984 in of the longer side of the fire tray sections and weld the 200 mm/ 7.874 in and 300 mm/ 11.811 in lengths of flat bar to the sides. Bend 25 mm/ .984 in of the 250 mm x 275 mm/ 9.842 in x 10.826 in section to form a ridge which you can hook into the barbecue. Tack weld the back between the sides.

BELOW RIGHT

Weld the 1,2 m/ 3 ft 11.244 in-long bar to the back of the barbecue, as shown, and hook the fire tray onto it. The six 600 mm/ 1 ft 11.622 in lengths of flat bar must also be welded to the inside of the unit, three on either side, so that they line up with the metal welded to the outside of the fire tray. See also page 61.

ABOVE LEFT
Bend the flue sections at 90 degrees and weld them together to form a square tube. The 350 mm/ 1 ft 1.779 in-long flat piece of metal is welded from corner to corner at the top of the flue, as it was for the fireplace. Weld the short piece of pipe to the center of this piece of metal. This is where the swivel hinge on the cowl will slot onto the flue. Use an angle grinder to smooth the rough edges.

CENTER RIGHT
Bend the edges on the sides of the cowl as indicated and weld the beak to the cowl.

ABOVE CENTER RIGHT
The barbecue grid is made with expanded metal and round bar, which is welded to the sides of the mesh and down the middle.

CENTER LEFT
The cowl slots neatly onto the top of the flue.

BELOW CENTER RIGHT
The grid slides onto the flat metal bar on one side of the fire tray and the metal bar on the other side of the barbecue.

BELOW LEFT
If you want to include the front shelf in your barbecue design, weld the hinges to one side of each section and fit it before you install the grid and fire tray. All the edges of these front sections must be bent as indicated in the drawings.
Then weld the 40 mm/ 1.574 in-long pieces of 10 mm/ .393 in bar to the two corners opposite the hinged side. Weld small pieces of flat bar together to create two L-shaped hooks and weld these to the front of the barbecue, at the bottom corners.

BELOW RIGHT
The round bar slots into the hooks and keeps the metal in place.

GLOSSARY

Alloy A substance composed wholly or mainly of metals, and usually combining several different metals. Brass is an alloy of copper and zinc; bronze is an alloy of copper and tin; cast iron is an alloy of iron, carbon and silicon.

Base metal The metal being welded or cut. Also known as the parent metal.

Brazewelding A process which produces high strength joins and is commonly used for repair work.

Brazing Process similar to hard soldering, often used to join different types of metal together with a non-ferrous filler material.

Butt joint A join where two pieces have been welded together in the same plane.

Carburising flame Gas welding or cutting flame which contains too much acetylene or other gas. Also referred to as a carbonising flame.

Duty cycle The amount of continuous time, in 10 minute cycles, that an arc welding machine can run before it needs to cool down. This is expressed as a percentage at a given amperage output.

Electrode The conductor through which electricity connects with the metal to create an electrical arc.

Fabrication General term used when referring to construction or manufacture of items from metal elements.

Ferrous metals Metals containing iron, such as wrought iron, carbon steel (including mild steel) and stainless steel.

Filler The various metals and materials which are added to metal joints during the various welding processes, such as electrodes, solder, flux and various brazing alloys.

Fillet joint A join which features a triangular shaped weld inside the 90 degree angle where two pieces of metal meet.

Flashback Reverse flow of burning gas within an oxy-acetylene torch, resulting in an audible backfire.

Flux A chemical compound used to clean metal prior to brazing or welding. It also reduces the formation of oxides on the metal when it is heated.

Forging Process used to shape metal by heating in a fire (forge) and by hammering.

Galvanising Process used to coat metal to protect it from rust. Hot dip galvanising involves dipping metal into zinc heated to a molten state; electro-galvanising involves coating the metal with silver.

Gas welding Welding process which uses a pressurized gas fuel such together with pressurized oxygen to heat the metal to be joined. A hand-held filler material (electrode or welding rod) is also used.

Gouging A process used to prepare metal for welding and to remove cracks and unwanted metal after welding steel.

Groove weld The weld is made in a groove between pieces. The groove may be square, beveled or U-shaped.

Heat affected zone (HAZ) The part of the metal which is heated (and subsequently cooled) during the welding process.

Inert gas A non-reactive gas such as argon or helium; used for welding processes such as MIG and TIG welding.

Jig Contraption used as a guide for cutting and bending of materials; also used to hold metal while working.

Lap join When two pieces in the same plane overlap. These are then joined using a fillet weld. The strongest lap join is welded on both sides.

Manual metal arc (MMA) welding Welding process that uses an electric arc to heat and fuse the metal together.

Metal inert gas (MIG) welding Welding process that uses a wire electrode/filler housed within the machine. During the process, an inert gas is distributed over the weld area to shield the hot metal from oxygen. With the introduction of shielding gasses having active elements, such as oxygen and carbon dioxide (CO_2), MIG is not technically correct and the American Welding Society (AWS) has adopted the name Gas Metal Arc Welding - GMAW.

Non-ferrous metals Metals which do not contain iron, such as copper and aluminum.

Oxy-fuel Combination of pressurized oxygen and a pressurized fuel gas used for various welding and cutting processes.

Plate Flat metal thicker than 5 mm.

Riveting Process used to join metal plates using rivets.

Sharadizing Process which involves plating metal with zinc.

Sheet Flat metal thinner than 5 mm.

Slag Oxidized waste which forms as a coating over the weld bead and along the bottom edge of an oxy-fuel cut.

Solder The wire used for both soft and hard soldering and for brazing. It is made from various soft metals, often with a high percentage of tin.

Soldering Process used to join the edges of less fusible metals. Soft and hard soldering is executed at lower and higher temperatures respectively, and for dissimilar metals.

Spatter Waste metal that splashes around the weld during welding.

Tungsten inert gas (TIG) welding A 'non-consumable' arc welding technique which uses a tungsten electrode that does not melt.

Verdigris Green patina produced by natural oxidisation on metal surfaces.

Weld bead Seam between two pieces of metal that have been joined by one of the welding processes.

TABLES

Please Note: these tables are not extensive but relate to the information supplied and used in this book

Imperial inches	Decimal inches	Metric mm
1/16	0.0625	1.1906
1/8	0.1250	3.1750
3/16	0.1875	4.7625
1/4	0.2500	6.3500
5/16	0.3125	7.9375
3/8	0.3750	9.5250
7/16	0.4375	11.1125
1/2	**0.5000**	**12.7000**
9/16	0.5652	14.2875
5/8	0.6250	15.8750
11/16	0.6875	17.4625
3/4	0.7500	19.0500
13/16	0.8125	20.6375
7/8	0.8750	22.2250
15/16	0.9375	23.8125
1	**1.0000**	**25.4000**
1 1/16	1.0625	26.9875
1 1/8	1.1250	28.5750
1 3/16	1.1875	30.1625
1 1/4	1.2500	31.7500
1 5/16	1.3125	33.3375
1 3/8	1.3750	34.9250
1 7/16	1.4375	36.5125
1 1/2	**1.5000**	**38.1000**
1 9/16	1.5625	39.6875
1 5/8	1.6250	41.2750
1 11/16	1.6875	42.8625
1 3/4	1.7500	44.4500
1 13/16	1.8125	46.0375
1 7/8	1.8750	47.6250
1 15/16	1.9375	49.2125
2	**2.0000**	**50.8000**
2 1/16	2.0625	52.3875
2 1/8	2.1250	53.9750
2 3/16	2.1875	55.5625
2 1/4	2.2500	57.1500
2 5/16	2.3125	58.7375
2 3/8	2.3750	60.3250
2 7/16	2.4375	61.9125
2 1/2	**2.5000**	**63.5000**
2.9/16	2.5625	65.0875
2 5/8	2.6250	66.6750
2 11/16	2.6875	68.2625
2 3/4	2.7500	69.8500
2 13/16	2.8125	71.4375
2 7/8	2.8750	73.0250
2 15/16	2.9375	74.6125
3	**3.0000**	**76.2000**

Wire Gauge

US Steel wire Gauge N°	Diameter in	mm
10	0.1350	3.4290
11	0.1205	3.0607
12	0.1055	2.6797
13	0.0915	2.3241
14	0.0800	2.0320
15	0.0720	1.8389
16	0.0625	1.5875
17	0.0540	1.3716
18	0.0475	1.2065
19	0.0410	1.0414
20	0.0348	0.8839
21	0.0317	0.8052
22	0.0286	0.7264
23	0.0258	0.6553
24	0.0230	0.5842
25	0.0204	0.5182

Ounces	Grams
1	**28.350**
2	56.699
3	85.049
4	113.40
5	141.75
6	170.10
7	198.45
8	226.80
9	255.15
10	283.50
11	311.84
12	340.19
13	368.54
14	396.89
15	425.24
16	453.59
17	481.94
18	510.29
19	538.64
20	566.99

NB. 1000 grams = 1 Kilogram

MATERIALS
– fireplace –
(Metric sizes)

Mild steel sheet:
3 mm, cut according to the illustrations for the fireplace;
2 x 1,2 m x100 mm for the flue;
1 x 500 mm x 500 mm for the ashtray;
1 x 500 mm x 500 mm for the cowl
Mild steel flat bar:
2 x 470 mm; 1 x 380 mm;
2 x 285 mm; 1 x 212 mm
[25 mm x 5 mm] for the trim;
2 x 480 mm; 1 x 390 mm;
2 x 295 mm; 1 x 222 mm [25 mm x 5 mm];
2 x 20 mm [10 mm x 5 mm] for the screen;
1 x 200 mm [25 mm X 5 mm] for the flue;
1 x 400 mm; 7 x 450 mm;
2 x 380 mm; 1 x 340 mm;
1 x 260 mm [52 mm x 5 mm] for the grate.
Mild steel round bar:
1 x 230 mm [5 mm] for the screen handle
Mlld steel square bar:
1 x 450 mm [10 mm x10 mm] for the grate
Mild steel flat bar with swivel hinge:
1 x 220 mm [25 mm x 5 mm]
Mild steel diamond mesh:
900 mm x 450 mm
[25 mm x 12 mm]

See Imperial sizes on page 55

MATERIALS
– barbecue –
(Metric sizes)

Mild steel sheet:
.118 in cut according to the drawings on page 59
2 x 4 ft 11.055 in x 1 ft 11.622 in for the flue
Expanded metal:
2 ft 10.252 in x 1 ft 10.440 in
Mild steel round bar:
2 x 2 ft 10.252 in;
3 x 1 ft 10.440 in;
1 x 1.574 in [.314 in]
Mild steel pipe:
1 x 3.937 in [.393 in internal diameter]
Mild steel flat bar:
1 x 3 ft 11.244 in;
6 x 1 ft 11.622 in;
1 x 1 ft 1.779 in;
2 x 11.811 in;
2 x 7.874 in [.984 in x .196 in]
Flat bar with swivel hinge:
1 x 8.661 in [.984 in x .196 in]
Hinges:
2 (optional)

*See Imperial sizes
on page 58*

Pressure Conversion Table

psi		Kpa	BAR	Atm
1	------	6.8948	0.06895	0.06805
10	------	68.948	0.6895	0.6805
20	------	137.869	1.379	1.361
30	------	206.844	2.0685	2.0415
40	------	275.792	2.758	2.722
50	------	344,74	3.4475	3.4025
60	------	413.688	4.137	4.083
70	------	482.636	4.8265	4.7635

INDEX

numbers in bold italics refer to captions

www.ingramcontent.com/pod-product-compliance
Lightning Source LLC
Chambersburg PA
CBHW061354090426
42739CB00002B/21